StarTribune

Sid Hartman's
GREAT MINNESOTA SPORTS MOMENTS

StarTribune

Sid Hartman's
GREAT MINNESOTA
SPORTS MOMENTS

with Joel A. Rippel

Voyageur Press

First published in 2006 by Voyageur Press, an imprint of MBI Publishing Company, Galtier Plaza, Suite 200, 380 Jackson Street, St. Paul, MN 55101-3885 USA

MBI Publishing Company titles are also available at discounts in bulk quantity for industrial or sales-promotional use. For details write to Special Sales Manager at MBI Publishing Company, Galtier Plaza, Suite 200, 380 Jackson Street, St. Paul, MN 55101-3885 USA

Editor: Josh Leventhal
Designer: Mandy Iverson

Printed in China

Library of Congress Cataloging-in-Publication Data

Hartman, Sid, 1920-
  Sid Hartman's great Minnesota sports moments / Sid Hartman with Joel Rippel.
    p. cm.
  ISBN-13: 978-0-7603-2656-5 (hardbound w/ jacket)
  ISBN-10: 0-7603-2656-8 (hardbound w/ jacket)
  1. Sports--Minnesota--History. I. Rippel, Joel A., 1956- II. Title. III. Title: Great Minnesota sports moments.
  GV584.M65H37 2006
  796.09776--dc22
                              2006016659

On the front cover: The Minnesota Twins celebrate victory following the 1987 World Series.

On the back cover (left to right): Andrew Brunette, Carl Eller, Thomas Vanek, George Mikan, Chris Carter.

On the title page: The University of Minnesota men's hockey team celebrated its second consecutive title in 2003.

Contents

Introduction
by Joel Rippel

In the 1940s, the two biggest things in the Twin Cities sports scene were the state high school basketball tournament and University of Minnesota football.

The three-day basketball tournament was the largest one-class high school tournament in the United States, routinely filling the 18,000-seat Williams Arena on the University of Minnesota campus.

Across the street from Williams Arena was Memorial Stadium, which was also regularly filled to watch the Gophers football team, which had won five national titles in an eight-year span (1933–41).

During this time, a young reporter was beginning his journalism career at the *Minneapolis Times*. The newspaper career of Sid Hartman got started just as some civic leaders began thinking about making the Twin Cities "big league."

"[*Minneapolis Times* sports editor] Dick Cullum told [circulation manager] Louie Mohs that he needed a young guy in the sports department. Mohs said 'I've got the guy for you,'" Hartman recalls. "Cullum knew me because I had been hanging around for years. Cullum said, 'Why not?' and he hired me."

Hartman, whose only previous newspaper experience was at the *Lincoln Life*, the student newspaper at Minneapolis North High School, was hired for $11.50 per week.

"Cullum is the guy who gave me my opportunity," Hartman said. "If not for him, I would have had a career selling vacuum cleaners."

Sid Hartman as a young reporter at WCCO radio in the late 1950s.

Hartman's first by-lined article in the *Minneapolis Times* appeared on November 1, 1944. The story, which was a preview of that weekend's University of Minnesota–Northwestern football game, was headlined, "Higgins run, stopping of win streak top Gopher-Wildcat games."

Less than a year after starting at the *Times*, Hartman began writing a column. Hartman's column appeared for the first time on September 13, 1945.

"Cullum always told the story that my column started when he couldn't make it to the office because of a snowstorm and he stuck my column in the paper," Hartman said. "Actually what happened was Cullum said, 'You have all of these notes that we can't get in the paper anywhere else. Start rounding them up and we'll run a column.'"

For years, that was the name of the column: "Hartman's Roundup."

In early 1948, the *Times* folded. But Hartman wasn't out of work for long. He was immediately hired by Charles Johnson, the executive sports editor of the *Minneapolis Star* and the *Minneapolis Tribune*.

"Charlie called me the first night and said, 'Come on down tomorrow. You're working for the *Star* and *Tribune*. We'll take care of you,'" Hartman said. "Joe Hendrickson was the sports editor of the *Tribune* and his plan was to put me on the desk. The *Tribune* managing editor, Dave Silverman, went to Charlie and said, 'You're bringing in the best reporter in town and putting him on the desk? What sense does that make?' The next day I was assigned to cover the Gophers." Hartman's first by-line in the *Minneapolis Tribune* appeared on May 16, 1948.

In 1955, Hartman was hired by WCCO radio. During the 1960s, while writing six columns per week for the *Tribune*, Hartman also served as the paper's sports editor. In 2003, Hartman received the Curt Gowdy Award from the Naismith Memorial Basketball Hall of Fame for his lifetime contributions to basketball.

In November 2004, Hartman celebrated his sixtieth anniversary with the newspaper, and in the summer of 2005, he celebrated his fiftieth anniversary with the radio station.

Through the years, Hartman's career has been highlighted by his scoops and his close personal friends.

Hartman, who played a significant role in the early campaign to bring major league sports to the Twin Cities, remains a strong voice to keep the Twin Cities "big league."

Hartman gets the inside scoop from Twins infielder John Castino in the early 1980s.

A true icon in the Minnesota sports and journalism scene, Sid Hartman was honored with his own bobble-head likeness in 2001.

chapter 1

BASKETBALL

Lakers in the Land of Ten Thousand Lakes:
The Birth of Professional Basketball in the Twin Cities

Professional basketball in the 1940s was a far cry from what it is today. Several, mostly regional, leagues were competing with one another for the fans' attention and the nation's top players. The twelve-team National Basketball League (NBL), formed in 1937, was based around the Midwest and Great Lakes region, with teams in smaller cities and towns like Sheboygan, Wisconsin; Oshkosh, Wisconsin; Fort Wayne, Indiana; and Indianapolis, Indiana. The forerunner of today's NBA, the Basketball Association of America (BAA), was established in 1946 in larger cities like New York, Boston, Philadelphia, and Washington, D.C., with teams playing in larger arenas. The oldest league, the American Basketball League, had been around since 1925, but it lost several franchises to the BAA after World War II.

Conditions in the newspaper business were a lot different back then as well. Everybody in the sports department had moonlighting jobs because sports writing didn't pay much. One did publicity for the Minneapolis Millers baseball team, one was a boxing referee, and another was a boxing promoter.

George Mikan battles Arnie Risen of the rival Rochester Royals at the Minneapolis Auditorium in 1954.

I got the idea of starting a professional basketball team. Minnesota didn't have any big-league sports then, so my boss Charlie Johnson, the executive sports editor, encouraged me to pursue a team.

In 1946, I read a story in the *Milwaukee Journal* about how successful the Oshkosh and Sheboygan teams had been. I met the owner of the Oshkosh team. He wanted to play an exhibition game in Minneapolis, but they needed a sponsor.

I convinced local businessman Ben Berger to promote the exhibition game between Oshkosh and Sheboygan at the Minneapolis Auditorium. The game, played on December 1, 1946, drew more than 5,000, and Berger got excited about the possibility of regular pro basketball in the Twin Cities. So I went looking for a franchise.

At first, a group owning the Youngstown team in the NBL was approached. They agreed to sell and then changed their minds. Later, in early 1947, I read in one of the Detroit papers that the Detroit Gems of the National Basketball League was available.

I went to local businessman Morris Chalfen and said, "I think we can get this team for $15,000." He said he didn't want to be the lead investor. So I went to Berger, who agreed to chip in.

I called the Gems owner, Morris Winston, to see if he wanted to sell. They had finished with the worst record in the NBL by winning just four games out of forty-four, and hadn't drawn any fans. He said he wanted $20,000. I said, "I'll get you $15,000." I flew to Detroit with the check. I was scared to death

The three main figures in the growth of the Minneapolis Lakers: George Mikan, Max Winter, and Ben Berger.

Jim Pollard joined the Lakers in 1947 and remained with the team until he retired as a player in 1955.

that I'd lose the money—it was the most money I'd ever had. Winston met me at the airport and we made the deal.

The deal was announced on June 3, 1947, and I was involved with the team for the next ten years.

George Barton wrote in the *Minneapolis Tribune* that he was doubtful whether pro basketball would be successful in Minneapolis because high school and college basketball were so popular. Gophers basketball was selling out, and high school basketball would sell out the 9,200-seat Minneapolis Auditorium for Friday doubleheaders.

All we got for the $15,000 paid for the Gems was a bunch of old uniforms and the contracts of six players. We ended up with only one player from Detroit, center Bob Gerber. The first move we made was in mid-August when we purchased the contracts of former Gophers Tony Jaros and Don "Swede" Carlson from the Chicago Stags of the BAA for $25,000. We also signed three other former Gophers: Don Smith, Ken Exel, and Warren Ajax.

Berger and Chalfen offered the team's general manager post to Minneapolis businessman Max Winter, who owned a bar/café and was a boxing and sports promoter. Winter accepted, and he ran the team for the next few years.

When we went looking for a coach, we first went after Hamline's Joe Hutton. We offered him a lot of money. But he wanted to stay at Hamline because his son—future Laker Joe Hutton Jr.—was going to play for him. Hutton coached at Hamline University for thirty-five seasons (1930–65).

Our next choice was John Kundla. A former Gophers player in the 1930s, Kundla was coaching at St. Thomas College. I went over to see him five times in a span of

ten days. We offered him a three-year contract that was guaranteed at $9,000 per year. He finally accepted, and Kundla stayed with the team for more than a decade.

Besides the uniforms and the contracts, we acquired one other crucial thing from Detroit: Because the Gems had finished in last place the previous year, we got the first pick in a dispersal draft. We used that pick to take George Mikan. Mikan had been with the Chicago American Gears of the Professional Basketball League of America (PBLA), which folded just two weeks into the 1947–48 season. The Gears first tried to be admitted to the NBL, but the league turned them down. The NBL then held a dispersal draft for the 160 players from the PBLA.

Jim Pollard was another one of the nation's top players at the time. He had won an NCAA championship with Stanford in 1942 and then went on to play for the U.S. Coast Guard for three years. After the war, Pollard joined up with

Coach John Kundla instructs his young Laker squad.

an amateur team called the Oakland Bittners. Several pro teams had tried to sign Pollard, but he liked playing for the amateur team and hoped to play for the U.S. Olympic team in 1948. We offered Pollard $12,000, and we got him as part of a package deal by signing him and two of his Oakland teammates, Bill Durkee and Paul Napolitano.

Once we signed Mikan too, the whole perception about the team and the league changed. The Minneapolis Lakers were a popular attraction in the Twin Cities within just a few months. By January, they were selling out the Minneapolis Auditorium.

With Winter and Kundla at the helm, and Mikan and Pollard as the cornerstones of the Lakers front court, Minneapolis would be a force to be reckoned with for the better part of the next decade.

The Minneapolis Lakers celebrated their first championship after the 1947–48 season.

The Rise and Fall of the NBA's First Dynasty

Before there was Shaquille O'Neal, Kareem Abdul-Jabbar, Wilt Chamberlain, or Bill Russell, basketball's first dominating big man played in the Twin Cities. George Mikan of the Minneapolis Lakers not only helped bring five basketball championships to the state of Minnesota, but he helped to put professional basketball on the national map.

The Minneapolis Lakers won the National Basketball League championship in the team's first year of existence by finishing with a 43-17 record in the 1947–48 season. Mikan, who scored 16 points in his debut for the Lakers, averaged 21.3 points per game during the season and earned first-team all-league honors. Pollard chipped in with 12.9 points per game. In the playoffs, the Lakers defeated Oshkosh and Tri-Cities to advance to the league finals. But before taking on Rochester in the NBL finals, the Lakers traveled to Chicago to play in the World Pro Tournament. The Lakers won three games in four days to win the tournament. In the championship game, Mikan scored 40 points to lead the Lakers to a 75-71 victory over the New York Rens and Sweetwater Clifton, who would later play for the Harlem Globetrotters. The Lakers then defeated Rochester, three games to one, in a best-of-five series to claim their first title.

Just as the Lakers were making their presence felt with the impressive inaugural season, the commissioner of the Basketball Association of America, Maurice Podoloff, tried to put the NBL out of business by inviting the franchises from Fort Wayne and Indianapolis to join the BAA at no cost. This move would have killed the NBL, leaving the Lakers in a minor league that would have folded sooner or later.

Max Winter, through one of his New York friends, had heard about Podoloff's move. At a meeting in Chicago during the summer of 1948, Winter was at his best—he persuaded Knicks president Ned Irish, Celtics owner Walter Brown, and the other BAA bigwigs to also take the Lakers and the Rochester Royals into the BAA. The four NBL teams merged with the BAA to form a twelve-team league for the 1948–49 season; the league was renamed the National Basketball Association the next year.

Mikan gave the Lakers immediate credibility. With his presence in the lineup, the Minneapolis team drew big crowds wherever they went. When the Lakers played the Knicks in New York's Madison Square Garden, the marquee read: "Geo. Mikan vs. Knicks."

Mikan led the league in scoring during the 1948–49 season, and he led the Lakers in assists as well. The team

Vern Mikkelsen, shown here in action during the 1958–59 season, was a Lakers star throughout the 1950s.

finished the regular season in second place, but they advanced to the BAA Finals. They defeated the Washington Capitals, four games to two, and claimed the BAA title.

The following year, the Lakers tied Rochester for the regular-season division title. Both Mikan and Pollard were named to the All-NBA First Team, with Mikan again leading the league in scoring. Minneapolis went on to win the NBA title in 1950—totaling three titles in three different leagues in three consecutive seasons.

The Lakers vs. the Globetrotters

The NBA wasn't very big in the late 1940s and early 1950s. The Lakers drew well here, but when they went into New York to play the Knicks, the game might draw only 5,000 or 6,000 people.

Around this time there was an annual basketball tournament held in Chicago for all professional teams. In addition to participants from the NBL, the tournament featured two all-black teams, the New York Rens and the Harlem Globetrotters.

Globetrotters owner Abe Saperstein decided it would be good for the Lakers to play the Globetrotters since they were the two best teams around. The Globetrotters had the best black players in the country, including Inman Jackson, Sonny Boswell, Sweetwater Clifton, and Marques Haynes.

One of the biggest problems was that Saperstein insisted on using his own officials from Chicago.

The teams played for the first time in February of 1948 in Chicago. The Globetrotters beat the Lakers by two points in the first game. After that, the Lakers demanded that the games have neutral officials. They played in Chicago again a year later, and the Globetrotters won again. Those two games drew the biggest crowds in the history of Chicago Stadium.

After the Globetrotters won those first two games, the Lakers won the next five games between the two teams over the next few years. They played one last time, in 1958, and the Lakers won.

When the games were held in Minneapolis, they played at the Auditorium. People lined up at three o'clock in the morning for tickets for that game. It was the darndest thing I've ever seen.

Saperstein actually helped to keep the NBA alive during that period with doubleheaders. The Globetrotters would play the first game, and then two NBA teams would play the second game. The Globetrotters' game would outdraw the NBA teams, so the league switched the order for the Globetrotters to play in the second game.

Abe Saperstein was a true basketball pioneer with his Harlem Globetrotters.

The Globetrotters-Lakers matchups were a big draw in the early 1950s. The Lakers won this contest, 72-68, in Chicago in February 1951.

Clyde Lovellette spent the first four seasons of his Hall of Fame career in Minneapolis.

The only year that the Lakers didn't win a title in their first six seasons was 1951. The team finished with the league's best regular-season record, and Mikan, Pollard, and Vern Mikkelsen all represented Minneapolis in the NBA's inaugural All-Star Game on March 2, 1951. However, the season came to a disappointing end after Mikan hurt his ankle and was slowed down in the playoffs. The Lakers lost to their biggest rival, the Rochester Royals, which went on to win the championship.

As dominant as Mikan was, he was only part of what was a truly great team. To this day, the best basketball games I have ever seen were the ones between the Lakers and Rochester during that era. The Lakers starting lineup included Mikan, Mikkelsen, Pollard, point guard Slater Martin—all Hall of Famers. The Royals had several star players of their own, such as Bobby Davies, Bobby Wanzer, Arnold Johnson, Arnie Risen, Red Holzman, and Jack Coleman.

In 1949, the addition of Vern Mikkelsen was a big help for the team's established stars Mikan and Pollard. Mikkelsen was selected by the Lakers in the first round of the 1949 draft as a territorial choice out of St. Paul's Hamline University.

Today, most NBA teams have big front lines, but the Lakers were the first team in pro basketball to play the three big men together: Mikan was six-foot-ten and Pollard and Mikkelsen both measured in at six-foot-seven. Coach Kundla was reluctant to play the three at once. He preferred to use Mikkelsen as a backup to Mikan, but Winter convinced him to keep Mikkelsen in the starting lineup, even after he got off to a slow start in 1949.

Mikkelsen eventually adjusted well to the NBA. He is considered the first true power forward in the history of the league. Minneapolis' big lineup forced opposing teams to play three big men at the same time to try and stop the imposing Lakers.

After Mikan's injury left the team short in 1951, the Lakers were back as champions in 1952. They toppled the defending-champion Royals in the semifinals before defeating the New York Knicks in the finals.

Because they won the title, the Lakers picked last (tenth) in the 1952 NBA draft. With their first-round choice, they took Clyde Lovellette from the University of Kansas. The six-foot-nine All-American had led Kansas to the 1952 NCAA title, but the other NBA teams passed on him because they didn't think they would be able sign him. Since the Lakers already had Mikan, Pollard, and Mikkelsen in the front court, they didn't need immediate help and could afford to take a chance on Lovellette.

Lovellette played on the 1952 U.S. Olympic team—which won the gold medal at the Helsinki games—and then he played for the Phillips 66 AAU team instead of coming to the Lakers right away. He joined the Lakers for the 1953–54 season.

For the second year in a row, the Lakers finished with the best record in the league, and for the fourth time in five seasons, the Minneapolis Lakers were champions of the NBA.

The 1954 title was the team's last in Minneapolis. Following the season, Mikan retired at the age of thirty to become the general manager. As the Lakers struggled early in the 1955–56 season, Mikan ended his eighteen-month retirement and returned as a player in January 1956. Minneapolis reached the playoffs but lost to St. Louis. Mikan retired again after the season.

Mikan took over as the team's coach in 1957, but after they stumbled to a 9-30 record, Kundla stepped down as the general manager and returned to coaching. The Lakers missed the

The last Minneapolis Lakers championship team (left to right): Slater Martin, Pep Saul, Jim Holstein, Jim Pollard, Clyde Lovellette, George Mikan, Vern Mikkelsen, Dick Schnittker, Whitey Skoog, and Coach John Kundla.

playoffs that year—the only time during the thirteen seasons in Minneapolis that they didn't reach the playoffs.

Mikan's retirement was only the first nail in the coffin for the Minneapolis Lakers. In 1956, the team had a chance to make a trade that might have turned the team's fortune around. I brokered a deal with Red Auerbach, the coach and general manager of the Boston Celtics, to send Vern Mikkelsen to Boston for the rights to three players (Cliff Hagen, Frank Ramsey, and Lou Tsioropoulos), since the Celtics needed a center to join Bob Cousy and the rest of the team's rising stars.

By trading Mikkelsen, the Lakers surely would have finished in last place and earned the first pick in the draft. The prize in the draft that year was Bill Russell, an All-American center from the University of San Francisco.

Auerbach and I had agreed that Mikkelsen would report to the Celtics on February 15, 1956, which was the day of the trading deadline. A couple of days before the trade was to be announced, owner Ben Berger had lunch with a local sportscaster, Dick Enroth, who told him not to make the deal. Berger told me to call it off. I told him I would try, but also made it clear that if the deal had to be called off, I would end my association with the Lakers. The Celtics agreed to call off the deal.

That season Rochester finished with the worst record in the league. On draft day, the Royals passed on Russell and took Sihugo Green of Duquense University. St. Louis had the second choice and drafted Russell and then traded him to Boston. The Lakers drafted third and took Jim Paxson from the University of Dayton.

Paxson lasted only two seasons in the NBA, the Lakers never had another winning season in Minnesota, and Russell's Celtics became one of the greatest dynasties in sports history, winning eleven titles in thirteen seasons.

Then, as now, stadium issues were at the crux of the team's future. In the mid-1950s, the Lakers didn't really have a home. For the whole month of March, you couldn't get into the Minneapolis Auditorium because of all the booked shows and conventions such as the Sportsman's Show. The Lakers had to shuttle between the St. Paul Auditorium, Minneapolis Auditorium, and the Minneapolis Armory. If the Russell deal had been made, Morris Chalfen, one of the owners of the team, would have built a new arena.

We came close to moving the Lakers to Los Angeles then, but Berger instead sold the team to Bob Short and a local group of

Even after Mikan retired, the physical play of Pollard (with the ball) and Mikkelsen (setting the pick) defined Lakers basketball in 1955.

Bob Short (left) purchased the controlling interest in the Lakers from Ben Berger in April 1957.

Future Hall of Famer Elgin Baylor lit it up during the Lakers' last two seasons in Minnesota.

stockholders for $150,000. Short eventually bought out all of the investors.

In 1958, the Lakers were bolstered by rookie Elgin Baylor, whom they selected out of Seattle University with the first overall pick in the draft. Baylor averaged nearly 25 points and 15 rebounds per game during the 1958–59 season, and even though the team finished with a 33-39 record, Baylor helped carry the Lakers to the NBA finals for the first time since 1954. In the finals, the Lakers were swept by the Boston Celtics. Following the season, Kundla quit the Lakers to become the basketball coach at the University of Minnesota.

The 1959–60 season was the Lakers' last in Minneapolis. The season was highlighted by Baylor, who quickly had emerged as one of the top players in the league. Early in the season, Baylor scored sixty-four points in the Lakers' 136-113 victory over Boston in Minneapolis—breaking the NBA record of sixty-one points in a game, which was set by George Mikan against Rochester in 1952. Baylor averaged 29.6 points and 16.4 rebounds, but the Lakers went just 25-50 during the regular season. In the playoffs (six of the league's eight teams went to the playoffs in those days), they beat Detroit in the first round and then took a 3-2 lead against the St. Louis Hawks in the best-of-seven Western Conference finals. But the Hawks, who had Bob Pettit, came

back to win the last two games and clinch the series. The Lakers' final game in Minneapolis was a 117-96 loss to St. Louis in front of a Minneapolis Armory record-crowd of 7,544. Baylor scored thirty-eight points for the Lakers.

One month later, Short announced that he had reached a tentative agreement to move the team to Los Angeles. The NBA owners met in New York the next day, April 27, and voted, seven to one, against allowing the Lakers to move. They were worried about the increased travel costs. After the vote, the owners were told that Abe Saperstein, owner of the Harlem Globetrotters, had just announced the formation of the American Basketball League, and he was going to put teams in Los Angeles and San Francisco. The NBA owners re-voted and unanimously approved the Lakers' move.

It's amazing. Short bought the team for $150,000. The team was originally purchased for $15,000. Short eventually sold it to Jack Kent Cooke for about five million dollars. Jerry Buss bought the team for $67.5 million. In December 2004, *Forbes* magazine valued the Los Angeles Lakers at $510 million.

The NBA Returns to Minnesota

For nearly three decades after the Lakers departed in 1960, the only professional basketball in Minnesota was two brief stints with the short-lived American Basketball Association (ABA). With George Mikan serving as the league's first commissioner, the Minnesota Muskies were among the eleven original ABA teams in 1968. The Muskies reached the conference finals that first year, but attendance was poor, and they were relocated to Florida the following season. The Pipers moved from Pittsburgh to replace the Muskies in the Twin Cities in 1969, but the team stayed for only one season.

In 1984, Governor Rudy Perpich and Minneapolis businessman Harvey Mackay met with NBA Commissioner David Stern to discuss getting a team back in Minnesota.

Meanwhile, Minneapolis businessmen Marv Wolfenson and Harvey Ratner, after failing to buy the Twins from Calvin Griffith, turned their attention to the NBA. They first pursued the Milwaukee Bucks and then reached an agreement to buy the Utah Jazz, but both franchises were eventually purchased by local interests who wanted to keep the teams in their respective cities. So, Wolfenson and Ratner decided to go after an expansion team.

Wolfenson's and Ratner's two-year lobbying efforts paid off in April of 1987, when the NBA announced it would expand by four teams. Charlotte and Miami would join the league for the 1988–89 season, and Minnesota and Orlando would come on board before the 1989–90 season. The expansion fee was $32.5 million. The league told Wolfenson and Ratner that getting the franchise

Coached by former Laker Jim Pollard (far right), the ABA's Minnesota Muskies came to town in 1967.

Although some fans sat a long way from the action, the Timberwolves broke attendance records in their first season while playing at the Metrodome.

was contingent on construction of a new arena starting no later than September 1, 1988.

The Timberwolves played their first season at the Metrodome while the Target Center was being built, and the team set several NBA attendance records that year. They set the record for attendance at an exhibition game (35,156), and the Timberwolves' opening game at the Dome drew an NBA-record 35,427 fans. Even though they won only twenty-two games (which was better than the other three expansion teams), the Wolves drew more than one million fans—the first time an NBA team had done that—and averaged more than 26,000 fans per game.

The Wolves increased their win total to twenty-nine in their second season, but coach Bill Musselman was fired after that season. It would be six years before they won that many games again.

During the 1993–94 season, Wolfenson and Ratner put the franchise up for sale. After just five seasons in Minnesota, it seemed that the Timberwolves might move.

Wolfenson and Ratner were burdened with huge debt. In addition to difficulties in other segments of their business, the Target Center had cost $15 million more than they expected.

Connie Hawkins was the star of the short-lived Minnesota Pipers in 1968–69.

Point guard Pooh Richardson, the team's first draft pick, drives past Phoenix's Jeff Hornacek in early-season action in 1989.

Tony Campbell was the Wolves' top scorer in each of the team's first three seasons.

The Target Center was ready for action by the start of the Timberwolves' second season.

They had paid more than $100 million to build the Target Center and lost more than $25 million paying off the arena debt in the team's first four seasons.

After the announcement that the team was up for sale, a group from New Orleans that was headed by boxing promoter Bob Arum offered $152.5 million for the franchise. The agreement was announced on May 23, 1994. Right away, the league said the deal was suspect. The move was blocked when the NBA relocation committee rejected the offer because the New Orleans group didn't have the dates available in the Superdome or the finances to pay $152.5 million. The sale was formally killed when the NBA filed a lawsuit with the U.S. District Court in Minneapolis.

Fortunately, a local buyer, Mankato businessman Glen Taylor, stepped in and bought the Timberwolves for $88.5 million in August 1994.

In January of 1995, the city of Minneapolis bought the Target Center from Wolfenson and Ratner for $54 million. The city issued another $25 million worth of bonds to cover obligations.

Taylor officially took control of the Timberwolves in March 1995. The first thing he did was name Kevin McHale as vice president for basketball operations. At the same time, he named Flip Saunders as the general manager. McHale was a native of Hibbing, Minnesota, and he had played at the University of Minnesota before embarking on a Hall of Fame career in the NBA. Saunders had been a teammate of McHale's with the Gophers and then went on to a successful coaching career in college and the Continental Basketball Association.

After six losing seasons—and four coaches—the 1995 draft was going to be very important for the Timberwolves.

From "Da Kid" to "Big Ticket": The Kevin Garnett Era

In 1995, nineteen-year-old Kevin Garnett became the first player in twenty years to be drafted into the NBA straight out of high school.

The Minnesota Timberwolves had picks among the top ten in the draft in each of their first six seasons. Yet, they were never able to nab any true franchise players to build around. Players like Pooh Richardson, Luc Longley, Christian Laettner, Isaiah Rider, and Donyell Marshall all went on to have long NBA careers, but none were of the caliber to carry the rest of the team. That was about to change.

Minnesota had the fifth overall pick in the 1995 NBA draft. Most observers agreed that the top five available players were Maryland's Joe Smith, Alabama forward Antonio McDyess, North Carolina's Jerry Stackhouse and Rasheed Wallace, and Kevin Garnett, a high school senior in Chicago. When the Timberwolves' turn came around, they took Garnett.

Everybody thought it was risky to take a kid out of high school. It had been twenty years since a high school player (Bill Willoughby in 1975) went directly to the NBA.

The Minnesota Timberwolves were probably the ideal team for Garnett. Minneapolis is a smaller market compared to other NBA cities, so there was less media spotlight on the young player. Coming to Minnesota also gave Garnett the chance to work with Kevin McHale, a Hall of Famer and one of the best post players in NBA history. You have to give McHale a lot of credit. He really worked with KG from day one and helped him to develop as one of the game's greatest players. Garnett's work ethic is truly unbelievable.

McHale and Saunders brought Garnett along slowly. While limiting Garnett's minutes to under thirty per game during his rookie season, the T-Wolves won twenty-six games in the 1995–96 season. The following year, Garnett moved into a full-time starting role and played nearly forty minutes per game. The Wolves finished with an amazing 40-42 record and made their first playoff appearance in the team's eight-year history.

The 1997–98 season was the final year of Garnett's original three-year contract. Taylor was convinced that if he didn't sign KG to a new contract right away either the Chicago Bulls or the Denver Nuggets would try to sign him. Taylor wanted to be sure he made Garnett an offer he couldn't refuse.

Negotiations began in July 1997 and broke down in August when Garnett rejected the team's offer of $103.5 million for six years. They started negotiating again in September. In early October, Taylor signed Garnett to a

Flip Saunders was named as the head coach twenty games into the 1995–96 season, and he remained a fixture on the sidelines for ten seasons in Minnesota.

Minnesota brought Garnett along slowly, but he was an all-star by his second season.

six-year contract extension worth $125 million. At the age of twenty-one and after just two seasons in the league, Garnett had signed the richest deal by an athlete in a team sport. The deal was reached just six hours before an NBA deadline would have stopped negotiations between the two sides until the following July.

The contract put Taylor on the hot seat with other NBA owners and probably contributed to a lockout by the owners the next season. The deal was far more lucrative than six-year extensions signed by Portland's Rasheed Wallace ($80 million), Vancouver's Bryant Reeves ($65 million), Cleveland's Bob Sura ($32 million), and Utah's Greg Ostertag ($30 million). The league had nine teams lose money in the 1996–97 season, and many owners didn't understand how a small-market franchise like the Timberwolves could afford a contract like the one offered to Garnett.

While some of the league owners favored a "hard" salary cap or some form of revenue sharing, the owners wanted to reopen negotiations with the National Basketball Players Association over a new collective bargaining agreement. On July 1, 1998, the owners imposed a lockout because the players' share of revenue had exceeded the 51.8 percent agreed upon in the existing collective bargaining agreement. Teams ended up playing just fifty games in the 1998–99 season because the league and the players association weren't able to settle on a new agreement until January.

Even as Garnett asserted his place among the NBA's elite in the late 1990s and the Wolves established themselves as a perennial playoff team, they couldn't amass the firepower to make it past the first round of the playoffs. Emerging superstar point guard Stephon Marbury forced a trade early in his third season with the team. Due to the league's new salary-cap restrictions, Garnett's hefty contract made it difficult to lure other high-priced stars to Minnesota.

In an effort to circumvent the cap rules, in early 1999 Glen Taylor signed free-agent forward Joe Smith to an illegal, secret contract. Under NBA rules, Smith could only sign one-year deals with the Wolves and not a long-term contract. The Wolves announced that they had signed Smith to a relatively modest one-year deal for $1.75 million. Yet in private, Smith's agent, Eric Fleisher, got Taylor to agree to a seven-year deal worth more than $80 million.

When the Wolves acquired Stephon Marbury on draft day in 1996, it looked as if he and KG represented the future of the organization. *AP/Wide World Photos*

Before long, the signing of Joe Smith was no laughing matter for the Timberwolves.

When the NBA found out about the secret deal—which came to light in October 2000 because of an unrelated lawsuit involving Fleisher—Commissioner David Stern fined the Timberwolves $3.5 million and stripped the team of its next five first-round draft choices. Stern also suspended Taylor and McHale. Everybody thought that losing the draft choices would kill the franchise.

I remember calling Stern at home on a Sunday afternoon shortly after he announced the Wolves' punishment. I had never heard him so upset. He was livid about the Wolves' actions. I think what made him so upset was that the league had just gone through tough negotiations for what he thought was a favorable collective bargaining agreement. He couldn't believe what Taylor and the team had done after he had done so much to prevent the Wolves from moving to New Orleans and had helped to find Taylor as the team's new owner.

Stern drew heavy criticism from a number of NBA officials about the severity of the punishment. He eventually restored two of the draft picks (2003 and 2005).

If the Timberwolves had wanted to cheat in signing somebody, they should have cheated on Stephon Marbury. Seriously though, for Glen Taylor, Kevin McHale, and the entire Timberwolves organization, the Joe Smith deal was obviously a huge setback.

Although the team bounced back with three fifty-win seasons between 2000 and 2003, the first-round hurdle in the playoffs remained insurmountable. In the summer of 2003, the Timberwolves made two major acquisitions by obtaining veterans Latrell Sprewell and Sam Cassell. Expectations were very high for the 2003–04 season.

With veteran stars in Sprewell and Cassell and an up-and-coming star in Wally Szczerbiak, the Wolves had a talented and deep squad playing alongside the "Big Ticket."

Kevin Garnett has risen to new heights as one of the league's best all-around players.

Right: KG 4 MVP.

The team responded with a franchise-best fifty-eight wins, and Garnett won the NBA's Most Valuable Player Award. He led the league in rebounding and finished third in points per game. Perhaps the most significant accomplishment was that the Minnesota Timberwolves won a playoff series in 2004. They won two, in fact, before losing to the Los Angeles Lakers in six games in the Western Conference Finals, despite injuries to Cassell and backup point guard Troy Hudson. If all the players had been healthy, they might have won the whole thing.

Left: Veteran guards Latrell Sprewell and Sam Cassell rejuvenated the Wolves in their run to the conference finals in 2004.

Wally Szczerbiak was an all-star in 2002, his third season in the league, but he was shipped to Boston in 2006.

The Wolves went into the 2004–05 season with everybody thinking they were going to be great once again. Many experts picked them to win the championship. But things didn't go well from the start. Taylor hit the nail right on the head when he said that the team was "just too comfortable." They didn't do anything with the roster during the off-season. During training camp, Sam Cassell wanted to renegotiate his contract, and Latrell Sprewell announced that he couldn't feed his family on $14 million per year. There were some questions about how hard they would play. Those issues, combined with injuries to Szczerbiak and Hudson during the season, just killed them. A season that began with dreams of a championship ended with their first missed playoffs in nine years.

I think McHale made a bad mistake when he fired coach Flip Saunders. His firing—which came on February 12, 2005, one day after a loss to Utah had dropped the Wolves' record to 25-26—was a shock. McHale and Saunders were close friends who had known each other since they were Gophers teammates in the 1970s. How do you fire a close friend? But McHale just thought Saunders wasn't tough enough. Garnett disagreed with the firing. He thought Saunders was the same coach he had been the previous season when the Wolves went 58-24, but he admitted that the team's focus wasn't the same as it had been the year before. I believe that if McHale had traded Cassell early in the 2004–05 season, the team wouldn't have had such a collapse and Saunders wouldn't have been fired.

Despite the frustrations and controversies that have surrounded Garnett, his status as a great player is undoubtable. Doug Collins—who coached Michael Jordan in Chicago—said Garnett is in the same class as Jordan because he can elevate his game like Jordan did. Garnett's massive contract extension may have altered the financial landscape for the sport of basketball, but it never affected Garnett's work ethic. In 2003–04, after signing another extension with the Timberwolves worth $100 million for five years, KG brought home the league's Most Valuable Player trophy.

Gophers Basketball:
From Conference Champions to a Program in Disgrace

Until the 1970s, the University of Minnesota basketball program had never seen the kind of success that Bernie Bierman and Murray Warmath brought to the football program, or that Dick Siebert had brought to Gophers baseball. For as long as it took to reach the top, it just as quickly hit bottom.

With the exception of the three wartime seasons in the mid-1940s, the Gophers basketball team had been coached by Dave McMillan from 1927 to 1948. In McMillan's eighteen seasons as coach, the Gophers won 196 games against 156 losses, with a shared Big Ten Championship in 1936–37.

When McMillan resigned as head coach in 1948, the university's athletic director, Frank McCormick, tried to hire John Wooden, who was in his second season as the coach at Indiana State University. Wooden wanted the Gophers job,

but a dispute over keeping McMillan on as an assistant became a sticking point. The university wanted to retain McMillan since he was still on the payroll, but Wooden wanted to bring in his own assistant. Wooden told McCormick that he needed a final answer in forty-eight hours because he was also being pursued by UCLA. When McCormick finally got approval by the university, he wasn't able to get in touch with Wooden. The phone lines were down due to a snowstorm. In the meantime, Wooden was offered the UCLA job, he accepted, and remained there for twenty-six seasons. McCormick was despondent over not being able to hire Wooden, who has repeatedly said he preferred the Minnesota job.

McCormick ended up hiring Ozzie Cowles. A Minnesota native, Cowles was the coach at the University of Michigan, which had won the Big Ten title in 1948. Before that, he had

Coach Dave McMillan, shown here in his final season, won nearly two hundred games with the Gophers.

Dave Weiss (left) and John Wallerius confer with Coach Ozzie Cowles before the season-opening game in 1950.

Cowles had some good clubs with the Gophers in his eleven years as coach. In his first season (1948–49), the Gophers went 18-3. That team had Bud Grant, Whitey Skoog, Jim McIntyre, Jerry Mitchell, and Harold Olson. In 1954–55 the Gophers went 17-5 and were the Big Ten runner-up. Cowles had six teams that finished third or better in the Big Ten, but he never won the league and never went to the NCAA tournament. (Of course, the NCAA tournament only had twenty-four teams back then.)

Cowles was fired after the 1958–59 season, and John Kundla was a natural to replace him. Kundla, who had played baseball and basketball for the Gophers in the late 1930s, had just stepped down as the coach of the Minneapolis Lakers after nearly twelve seasons in that position.

Kundla and his assistant Glen Reed did a good job of recruiting players to come to Minnesota. They also recruited the first black players to play for the university: Don Yates, Lou Hudson, and Archie Clark.

Hudson and Clark started and Yates was the sixth man for the Gophers in the 1963–64 season. The team went 17-7 and finished third in the Big Ten with a 10-4 record. The next season, all three were starters and the Gophers finished second with an 11-3 record in the conference. They were 19-5 overall, but again missed the NCAA tournament. Michigan, which had the great Cazzie Russell, was the only Big Ten team to play in the tournament in those years.

After Hudson and Clark left, Kundla was short of talent. The Gophers finished ninth in the Big Ten in 1967 and 1968, and Kundla stepped down following the 1967–68 season.

To replace Kundla, the university brought in Bill Fitch, who had just completed his first season as the coach at Bowling Green State University. Before that, he had coached for five seasons at the University of North Dakota. Fitch stayed at Minnesota for only two years before getting a job in the NBA, where he coached for twenty-five seasons.

One of the potential replacements for Fitch was Bob Knight. Knight had played at Ohio State and was coaching at Army, but he wanted a job in the Big Ten. Minnesota ended up giving the job to Fitch's assistant, George Hanson.

coached at Carleton College in Northfield, Minnesota, and at Dartmouth, which he led to the NCAA championship game in 1942.

McCormick didn't want to hire Cowles. But the *Tribune*'s sports editor Charlie Johnson and columnist Dick Cullum were in love with Cowles and wrote that McCormick should hire him. Cowles' athletic director at Michigan wanted to get rid of him.

Best known for his later career as a football coach, Bud Grant starred in basketball at the university.

John Kundla came over from the Lakers in 1959 to coach the Gophers.

Hanson only lasted one year, so I called Knight again to see if he'd be interested this time. By then, he was all set to take the Indiana job.

University athletic director Marsh Ryman hired Murray State's Cal Luther to take over as coach for the 1971–72 season, but Luther reconsidered and gave up the job the next day—which was the best thing that could have happened for Gophers basketball. Shortly after Luther backed out, Ryman hired the thirty-year-old Bill Musselman, who had been coaching at Ashland College in Ohio for six seasons.

Lou Hudson puts up a shot against the University of North Dakota in December 1965.

The Gophers basketball program had a good, if rocky, run under Coach Bill Musselman, shown here with members of the 1973–74 squad.

Interest in Gophers basketball was at a low point when Musselman took over. They had averaged more than 10,000 people per game just once in the previous eleven seasons, and only 6,500 over the previous four seasons. Before the first season under Musselman was over, the fans were packing Williams Arena. He started a great pre-game show, which he brought with him from Ashland, and the Gophers started winning too.

Musselman's first season was marred by a brawl in the game against Ohio State at Williams Arena. The brawl started with thirty-six seconds remaining in the game, and ended with Ohio State's Luke Witte being carried off the court. The game was stopped and Ohio State, which was leading 50-44 when the trouble began, was declared the winner. Big Ten commissioner Wayne Duke was in attendance at the game, and the brawl drew national attention from a story in the next issue of *Sports Illustrated*. Because of their role in the brawl, Gophers forwards Corky Taylor and Ron Behagen were suspended for the remainder of the season. An enraged Ohio State coach Fred Taylor blamed Musselman for the brawl.

Other than bringing in the controversial Behagen, who had a less-than-stellar reputation before coming to Minnesota, Musselman and his assistant Jimmy Williams brought in other talented athletes including Gophers baseball star Dave Winfield. They recruited Winfield from an intramural league

Senior forward Dave Winfield shoots a jumper against the University of Wisconsin–Milwaukee early in the 1972–73 season at Williams Arena.

The Ohio State–Minnesota game on January 25, 1972, turned ugly in the final minute of play.

on campus and he quickly moved into the starting lineup. Despite losing Taylor and Behegan, the Gophers won seven of their last nine games, finished with a record of 18-7 overall, and were 11-3 in the conference to win the 1971–72 Big Ten title. It was their first conference title in thirty-five years. The Gophers also played in the NCAA Tournament for the first time in school history. (They lost to Florida State.)

The Gophers' overall record improved to 21-5 in Musselman's second season, but they finished second to Indiana in the Big Ten with a 10-4 record. They missed the NCAAs and played in the NIT tournament that year.

In the 1973–74 season, the Gophers struggled to a 12-12 record, but Musselman put together his strongest group for the following season. The starters for 1974–75 included future NBA players Mychal Thompson, Mark Landsberger, and Mark Olberding; the guards were Dennis Shaffer and Flip Saunders. It appeared as though Musselman had a nucleus that could win a couple of Big Ten titles and maybe

Jim Dutcher coached the Gophers from 1975 to 1986 before leaving under the cloud of another scandal.

Bill Musselman

Bill Musselman is one of the best basketball coaches the state of Minnesota has ever had.

Musselman coached the Gophers for four seasons before resigning in 1975 to join the pro ranks as coach of the ABA's San Diego Sails. The Sails folded just eleven games into the 1975–76 season, and Musselman became the Virginia Squires coach—one of five people to hold that job during what would be the ABA's final season.

After the ABA, Musselman coached Reno of the Western Basketball Association for one season and then went on to coach the Cleveland Cavaliers of the NBA for parts of two seasons. After the brief stint with the Cavs, he coached in the Continental Basketball Association for five seasons and won four league titles. He coached the Albany Patroons to a 60-10 record in the 1987–88 season.

In 1988, he was named the coach of the expansion Minnesota Timberwolves.

While he was coaching the Timberwolves, Musselman had a meeting with team owners Marv Wolfenson and Harvey Ratner and team president Bob Stein. The team wasn't winning, and they asked Musselman, "Why aren't we playing the young guys?" They especially wanted Gerald Glass, the team's first-round draft choice in 1991, to play more. That night the team went out and won, but Musselman played the same guys. After the game, he said, "I did it my way."

Under Musselman, the Timberwolves won twenty-two games in their first season and twenty-nine in the second season, but Wolfenson and Ratner let Musselman go after just two seasons. It would be six more seasons before they won that many games again.

After leaving the Timberwolves, Musselman coached two seasons at South Alabama, taking them to the NCAA tournament in 1997. After that season, he became an assistant in the NBA again.

On May 5, 2000, Bill Musselman died of bone marrow cancer at the age of fifty-nine.

In four seasons at the university and two seasons with the Timberwolves, Bill Musselman was one of Minnesota's greatest basketball coaches.

Kevin McHale went on to a Hall of Fame career in the NBA after leaving the Gophers.

piece on Musselman for the *Minneapolis Star* that alleged recruiting violations. After the story ran, the NCAA began an investigation of the program.

Just as the investigation was getting started, Musselman left in July of 1975 to coach the San Diego Sails of the American Basketball Association. Landsberger and Olberding left the program when Musselman did. Landsberger transferred to Arizona State, and Olberding left school to sign with San Diego.

In 1976, the NCAA announced 126 rules infractions and placed the Gophers program on probation for three years. They also lost three scholarships for two years. A lot of the violations were minor, but there were several major infractions including boosters making payments to student athletes.

Jim Dutcher, who had been an assistant coach at Michigan, was brought in to replace Musselman. The Gophers were on probation during Dutcher's second and third seasons, and although the team went 24-3 in 1976–77, they were ineligible for the postseason. That squad featured a six-foot-ten freshman out of Hibbing, Minnesota, named Kevin McHale. Along with Mychal Thompson and "Sugar" Ray Williams, McHale was one of three future NBA first-round picks on the team.

Dutcher stayed on as coach for eleven seasons, including a Big Ten title in 1981–82—Minnesota's first conference championship in ten years. That team had players Randy Breuer and Trent Tucker. However, like Musselman before him, Dutcher left the university under the shadow of scandal.

In January of 1986, three Gophers basketball players were accused of sexual assault following a Gophers-Badgers game in Madison, Wisconsin. I thought Ken Keller, who was the president of the university at the time, acted much too quickly when he decided to forfeit the Gophers next game. Dutcher wanted to play the game, which was scheduled for a Sunday afternoon, and then he was going to hold a press conference on Monday to announce his resignation, effective at the end of the season. Dutcher wanted the university to be patient and see what happened in the court of law.

Keller should have given these kids a chance to go to court and get a fair trial, but he went ahead and forfeited the next game. Dutcher resigned immediately.

As it turned out, all three players were acquitted of the charges. But the damage had been done, and the program suffered another severe setback.

everybody predicted big things for the future. But those hopes were quickly dashed.

In 1975, there was a newspaper writer in town by the name of Chan Keith. He made up his mind that he was going to get Musselman, and he did an investigative

The Final Four That Never Was: Clem Haskins and More Gopher Scandals

The scandals surrounding the Gophers basketball team over the last thirty years cast a long shadow over the program, even when they emerged from the Musselman and Dutcher controversies to reach college basketball's Final Four in the 1990s.

When it came time to find a new basketball coach to replace Dutcher in 1986, the University of Minnesota vice president Frank Wilderson wanted to hire a black coach. He first talked to Temple coach John Chaney. Chaney didn't want the job, but he recommended Clem Haskins, who was the coach at Western Kentucky University. Wilderson went after Haskins, and he accepted the post.

Haskins came in and did a great job, especially considering all the problems that the program had to confront at the time.

After two losing seasons, Haskins got Minnesota back on track in 1988–89, when the Gophers' 19-12 record was good enough to earn them a trip to the NCAA tournament for the first time since 1982. They improved to 23-9 the following year and were back in the tournament. The Gophers advanced to the Elite Eight in the 1990 NCAA basketball tournament, thanks to an upset victory over number-two-seeded Syracuse in the Sweet Sixteen, before losing to Georgia Tech by two points.

The Gophers' best season under Haskins was 1996–97, when they went 27-3 in the regular season and won their first Big Ten title since 1982. They opened the season with five victories. After suffering their first loss, at Alabama, they won their next ten. After their second loss, they won twelve consecutive games. The Gophers earned a number-one seed in the NCAA tournament, and they beat UCLA for the Midwest Regional championship to earn their first trip to the Final Four. I think they could have beat Kentucky in the semifinals, and possibly won the NCAA championship, if they had been healthy. Junior guard Eric Harris was hurt, and Bobby Jackson, who eventually was named to the All-Tournament Team, was slightly injured too.

Following the 1998–99 season, Haskins became the third Gophers basketball coach since 1975 to leave the program amidst a major controversy. The roots of that controversy extended back nearly a decade.

Not long after Haskins came to Minnesota, a couple of coaching jobs had opened up around the country. The university had a choice of either losing Haskins to another

The Gophers struggled in their first season under Coach Clem Haskins, but within a few years they were winning consistently.

The Big Ten Title was a high point of Haskins' tenure. He celebrates here with his family.

Guards Bobby Jackson and Charles Thomas celebrate Minnesota's first trip to the NCAA Final Four following a win against UCLA in the Regional Final.

school or letting him hire his own academic advisor for the basketball program. Hiring his own advisor was something he had wanted ever since he had been unable to recruit seven-foot high school star Elmore Spencer because of academic reasons. The university allowed Haskins to hire Alonzo Newby to oversee the academic performance of the players.

I don't know how much Haskins knew about what was going on, but I know that Newby was scared to death of him. Newby had to make sure that all the players were academically eligible. A woman named Jan Gangelhoff was hired as a tutor, and it turns out she did a lot of cheating for the players.

I'm not condoning the cheating, of course, but in my opinion the trouble started when Haskins kicked guard Russ Archambault off the team in February of 1998 for violation of team rules. Both Archambault and Eric Harris were disciplined for being out late, but Haskins didn't kick Harris off the team. Gangelhoff was very close to Archambault, and from that day on she made up her mind that she was going to get Haskins—and she eventually got him.

In March of 1999, the *St. Paul Pioneer Press*, using Gangelhoff as its source, did a big investigative report on the Gophers basketball program and uncovered the academic scandal. In June, the university bought out Haskins' contract for $1.5 million. University of Minnesota president Mark Yudof thought it was in the school's best interest to buy out Haskins. He believed that the public had lost confidence in the program, and with an impending NCAA investigation, the school would be better off starting over with a new coach. Yudof had to make a change. The university was getting beat up in the media every day.

Later in 1999, university athletics department officials Mark Dienhart, Jeff Schemmel, and McKinley Boston were all fired. I think it was a mistake to fire them. I'm also told by insiders that the night before Yudof held the press conference to announce that he was firing those three guys, he told at least two regents that he was going to put them on probation and not fire them. At that time, it was said that Yudof believed Haskins did a lot of that stuff without their knowledge. In the end, they wiped the slate clean and let the three men go.

I think Boston had done a good job of establishing some important relationships with a lot of people on campus. He helped athletics and he helped get a lot of kids in school, and I believe the university suffered when he left.

Junior Sam Jacobson, of Cottage Grove, goes in for a lay-up against the Kentucky Wildcats during the 1997 Final Four.

In October of 2000, the NCAA announced the penalties for the Minnesota basketball program. In addition to putting the program on a four-year probation, the NCAA cut scholarships and limited the number of recruiting visits. Perhaps the biggest slap was eliminating from the record books the Gophers' 1997

University president Mark Yudof and McKinley Boston, vice president for Student Development and Athletics, address the Haskins scandal.

The fiery Dan Monson took over the scandal-plagued Gophers program in 1999.

Final Four appearance and 1998 NIT Championship. Both banners were removed from Williams Arena.

The guy that was brought in to pick up the pieces of the basketball program in the wake of the Haskins scandal was Gonzaga University's Dan Monson. Minnesota had wanted to hire Utah coach Rick Majerus, and they also talked to the Timberwolves' Flip Saunders, but neither was interested in the job. Other candidates were interviewed as well.

After spending more than a decade at a relatively small college program, Monson grabbed national attention when he led Gonzaga to the Regional Finals of the 1999 NCAA tournament, including a first-round upset victory over the University of Minnesota.

When Monson arrived at the university as the Gophers' new coach in the fall of 1999, the program was mired in sanctions for the next five years. I don't think he was very happy in the beginning. I don't think his family was happy either. He did stick around, though, and did an admirable job under the circumstances.

In the spring of 2002, after three seasons with the Gophers, Monson was offered the coaching job at the University of Washington. I think he would have accepted the offer if Washington had agreed to pay the buyout of Monson's Minnesota contract, which was about $350,000 or $400,000. I talked to Yudof one morning, and he told me, "He's gone."

Yet Monson stayed, and once the NCAA sanctions were over, he was on the spot. The Gophers went 21-11 in 2004–05 and made the NCAA tournament for the first time since 1999.

Chris Voelz and the Growth of Gophers Women's Basketball

Chris Voelz served as the director of athletics for women's sports at the University of Minnesota from 1988 to 2002, and she deserves much of the credit for the success and growth of women's athletics at the university, particularly in hockey and basketball. She also had more support than any other coach or athletic director during the long period I covered the university. The support came from some very influential people like Kathleen Ridder and John Cowles Jr. and his wife, who have contributed a great deal to the university and carried a lot of clout.

Perhaps Voelz's biggest accomplishment in the basketball program was not only hiring Pam Borton as the basketball coach

in May 2002, but also for forcing university president Mark Yudof and the administration to fire the previous coach, Cheryl Littlejohn, after the 2000–01 season.

Littlejohn still had one year remaining on her contract, and Yudof wasn't in the mood to pay off Littlejohn to hire a new coach. The athletic department had a lot of financial problems at the time.

Voelz had told one of the top Big Ten Conference officials that she was troubled with some of the rules violations in the women's basketball program, but didn't know how to handle it. Voelz found a way to get rid of Littlejohn. After the administration said no to firing Littlejohn, Voelz reportedly

Chris Voelz was instrumental to the success of the women's athletics program at the university in the 1990s.

Coach Brenda Oldfield got the women's basketball team on track in 2001.

informed the NCAA of all the violations, and Littlejohn's contract was terminated without final payment. The NCAA's investigator called the twelve violations "a major infractions case." Among the violations were giving $200 to $300 to a recruit, buying clothing for players, and holding practices before the official start date.

Voelz hired Brenda Oldfield (now Frese) to replace Littlejohn for the 2001–02 season. Oldfield really turned the program around. The team went from an 8-20 record in 2000–01 to 22-8 under Oldfield's leadership. The Associated Press named her the Women's Basketball Coach of the Year, but Oldfield left after the season to become the coach at the University of Maryland.

The hiring of Borton further pushed the program to new heights. Under Borton, the Gophers went 25-6 in the 2002–03 season and reached the Sweet Sixteen in the NCAA tournament. They opened the following season

The Gopher women have become an elite team under coach Pam Borton.

with fifteen consecutive wins en route to a final record of 25-9. Minnesota hosted the first two rounds of the 2004 NCAA Women's Basketball Tournament, and the Gophers went on to defeat number-one-ranked Duke University to advance to the Final Four for the first time in school history.

Littlejohn deserves some of the credit because she recruited Lindsay Whalen and Janel McCarville, the two players that led the Gophers to the Final Four in 2004. Whalen is the all-time leading scorer, male or female, in the history of Gophers basketball. As a sophomore, she was named Big Ten Player of the Year in 2002 and went on to be an All-American in 2003 and 2004. McCarville, who set an all-time NCAA tournament record in 2004 with seventy-five rebounds, was the number-one pick in the WNBA draft in 2005.

In addition to the successes on the hardwood, Chris Voelz deserves credit for the rise of the women's hockey program as well. She hired Laura Halldorson to start up the hockey program in 1997, and it's been one of the most successful in the nation. They've won three national titles under Halldorson, including back-to-back championships in 2004 and 2005.

Under Voelz's leadership, the women's athletics program got a new hockey arena, a new softball field, and a new soccer field. The Sports Pavilion was originally remodeled for the women, and they're going to get a $4.6 million rowing building.

But Voelz's fourteen-year tenure as the women's athletic director was marred by several high-profile lawsuits, tremendous turnover in the department, and poor morale. Then-University President Nils Hasselmo admitted Voelz's weaknesses when he appointed a facilitator to work with her when he announced her new five-year contract in May 1993.

By 2002, the University of Minnesota was just one of five NCAA Division I athletic programs that had separate athletic departments for men and women. During that spring, president Mark Yudof announced that the departments would be merged and that women's athletic director Chris Voelz and men's athletic director Tom Moe would not be retained. It was a move aimed at saving money because maintaining separate departments was costly and there were overlapping expenses. Yudof had held a

Lindsay Whalen drives past a defender during the 2004 Final Four. The dream season came to an end when the Gophers lost to the eventual-champion Connecticut Huskies.

Minnesota's dynamic duo in 2004: Lindsay Whalen and Janel McCarville.

Among her many contributions, Voelz worked hard to get an arena built for the women's hockey team. Ridder Arena was the first facility dedicated solely to women's hockey.

public meeting with forty speakers, and thirty-nine of them wanted to keep the athletic departments separate.

There was intense pressure on Yudof to keep Voelz. Rumors were circulating that she was going to sue the university if she were fired. But Yudof, who inherited a tough situation in the Gophers men's basketball academic fraud case, showed a lot of guts when he announced Voelz would not be retained.

Voelz's supporters were worried that the women's department would get shortchanged after the merger. In July 2002, Minnesota native Joel Maturi was hired as the first athletic director of the merged department. Maturi, who had been the athletic director at Miami (Ohio) University, has continued to maintain equality between the men's and women's athletic programs.

Coach Laura Halldorson led the Gopher women to back-to-back hockey titles in 2004 and 2005.

High School Basketball: The State Tournament

In 2003, in honor of the seventy-fifth anniversary of Williams Arena, the *Star Tribune* ran a list of the top seventy-five memories at the university's arena. In my opinion, nothing stands out more than when the Boys' State High School Basketball Tournament was just one class and held at Williams Arena.

In the 1950s, the tournament was the largest one-class basketball tournament in the country. Before the fire marshals got involved, Marsh Ryman, the Gophers' ticket manager who later became the athletic director, would find a way to get more than 18,000 fans in for every championship session. (The official capacity from 1950 to 1971 was 18,025.) Ryman got as many as 19,213 fans into the arena.

In those days, *Tribune* photographer John Croft and I used to travel to three or four cities whose teams had qualified for the tournament. We visited with the players and Croft took

The Minneapolis Auditorium was always packed for the state high school basketball tournament.

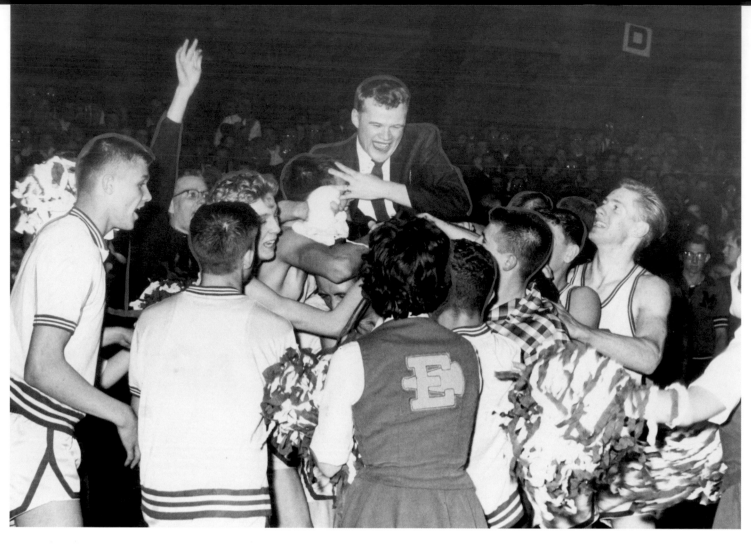

Coach Rich Olson and his Edgerton team celebrated a surprising tournament title in 1960.

photographs capturing the tournament fever in the towns. We never talked to a kid who didn't say his dream was to play in Williams Arena.

One of the greatest tournaments was in 1960 when tiny Edgerton defeated Austin for the state title. Coached by the twenty-three-year-old Richie Olson, who was in his first year of coaching, Edgerton was making its first-ever appearance in the state tournament. For Austin, coached by Ove Berven, it was the thirteenth appearance in twenty years. A crowd of 19,018—a record for a Minnesota high school basketball game—filled Williams Arena to watch the championship game. Edgerton won the game, 72-61.

In 1966, a great Edina team coached by Duane Baglien beat Duluth East, 82-75, to win the title in front of 18,696 fans. That was the first of three consecutive state titles for

Bob Zender helped to lead the Edina Hornets to three consecutive state titles from 1966 to 1968.

Edina's Duane Baglien coached the school to a record-setting sixty-nine-game winning streak in the late 1960s.

Although it doesn't attract the attention that it once did, the state basketball tournament still provides plenty of excitement. Just ask the boys from Hopkins, who won their second-straight Class AAAA title in 2006.

Edina—the first team in state history to win three in a row. Edina had a 79-1 record, which included a record 69-game winning streak, over that three-year span. The Edina team had great athletes like future Gopher and Viking Jeff Wright and Bob Zender, who was the most highly recruited player in Minnesota during the 1960s.

The last year of the one-class tournament was 1970, and it was one of the most memorable. Sherburn, led by Tom Mulso and Jeff McCarron, defeated the favored South St. Paul, 78-62, before 18,003 fans to win the title. Sherburn, which was making its first appearance in the state tournament, went into the championship game undefeated; South St. Paul had suffered just one loss. Mulso scored thirty-nine points in the championship game to lead the Raiders. The 1972 tournament was another classic, when St. James defeated Melrose for the Class A state title on Jeff Nessler's bank shot from forty feet at the buzzer.

In 1971, the tournament was split into two classes. That first two-class tournament drew 140,313, but attendance and interest have diminished ever since. The 2006 tournament, with four classes, drew just 67,002 fans.

What was once one of the greatest attractions in Minnesota sports was ruined. No more could you have the little towns like Sherburn and Edgerton come in and knock off the big city schools.

chapter 2

BASEBALL

Minor Leagues, Major Players: The Millers and Saints

For more than six decades prior to the existence of the Minnesota Twins, two minor league teams battled for Twin Cities baseball supremacy: the Minneapolis Millers and the St. Paul Saints. The origins of the two teams date to the late 1800s, and they had been rivals in the American Association since 1902.

In addition to playing each other twenty or more times throughout the year, the Millers and Saints also had a great holiday tradition that went back to the early years of the league. Every Memorial Day, July Fourth, and Labor Day, the Saints and Millers would play a split doubleheader, with one game played at Nicollet Park in Minneapolis and the other at Lexington Park in St. Paul.

The roster of players that at one time donned Millers or Saints uniforms includes some impressive names. In the early 1900s, the Millers included future Hall of Famers like Rube Waddell (in 1911–13) and Zack Wheat (in 1928). In 1938, the team was joined by a nineteen-year-old outfielder from San Diego named Ted Williams.

Minnesota Twins—1991 World Champions.

The Millers' home field, Nicollet Park, was small, just 279 feet to the right-field fence, and Williams hit a league-high forty-three home runs in his one season with the team, while also leading the Association with 142 runs batted in and a .366 batting average.

The Millers remained an independent minor league team from 1939 to 1945, when longtime owner Mike Kelley sold the team to the New York Giants. Kelley had been a central figure in Twin Cities baseball since the early twentieth century and worked in both the Saints and Millers organizations before buying the Millers in 1923, where he remained for the next twenty-three years.

When the Millers became the farm team for the Giants, it brought a new dimension to the rivalry with their cross-town foes. The Saints of St. Paul were affiliated with the Brooklyn Dodgers at the time, and the longstanding Giants-Dodgers rivalry was extended to the Twin Cities.

During the era of the Giants, the Millers featured future Hall of Famers Willie Mays, Hoyt Wilhelm, and Ray Dandridge. Mays only stayed in Minneapolis for a few weeks in 1951; the Giants quickly called up the young center fielder—his .477 average after thirty-five games was hard to resist. Wilhelm spent two seasons (1950–51) with the Millers before moving on to a twenty-one-year career in the majors. Although Ray Dandridge never made it to the big leagues, he had a Hall of Fame career in the Negro Leagues before becoming the first

Mike Kelley was a fixture in Minnesota baseball for half a century.

African American to play for the Millers in 1949. He was the American Association's most valuable player in 1950.

The Millers' final season at Nicollet Park came in 1955. Managed by future Twins skipper Bill Rigney, the team won the American Association regular-season title with a 92-62 record. They also hit an Association-record 241 home runs and included future Hall of Famer Monte Irvin and future Twins Billy Gardner and Al Worthington. The Millers reached the Junior World Series—a series between the champions of the American Association and the International League—for the first time since 1932. They defeated the Rochester Red Wings to win their first-ever Junior World Series title.

The Millers became an affiliate of the Boston Red Sox in 1958, when they were managed by another future Twins

Fans flocked to see the Millers play at Nicollet Park from 1896 until 1955.

The short distance to right field in Nicollet Park made a tempting target for Millers sluggers.

manager, Gene Mauch. The team finished in third place during the regular season, but they defeated Wichita and Denver in the playoffs to advance to the Junior World Series once again. The Millers beat the Montreal Royals to win their second title in four years.

In the following season, the Millers advanced to the Junior World Series to face the Havana Sugar Kings. After playing the first two games at Metropolitan Stadium in Bloomington, the series moved to Havana for the duration because it was too cold in Minnesota. The Sugar Kings were

Willie Mays, shown here with Phil Tomkinson, briefly roamed the outfield for the Millers in 1951.

Ted Williams was one of the many legends to grace the Nicollet Park field.

Don Zimmer was one of the many Dodgers prospects to get their start in St. Paul.

While serving as Boston's farm club, the Millers included Carl Yastrzemski and other future major leaguers.

A Saints player receives hearty congratulations after homering in a 1951 game at Lexington Park.

cheered on by Fidel Castro, who had taken power less than a year earlier, and they won the series in seven games.

Although the St. Paul Saints didn't have the success that the Millers had during this era, the club was graced by some superior talent. Future Hall of Famer Duke Snider got his start with the Saints in 1947, and Roy Campanella joined the team in May 1948. He broke the color barrier as the first African American player in the American Association. Another Hall of Famer, future Dodger skipper Walter Alston, managed the club in 1948 and 1949.

The Twin Cities Go Big League: Wooing the Senators

On April 21, 1961, nearly 25,000 fans gathered at Metropolitan Stadium in Bloomington to watch the Minnesota Twins take on the expansion Washington Senators in the first regular-season major league baseball game in the state. The hometown team lost that inaugural contest, but a new era in Minnesota sports had begun.

The road to making the Twin Cities major league was a long and bumpy one.

Prior to 1953, the Twin Cities had little hope of getting a major league baseball club. For fifty years, from 1903 to 1953, the American League and National League had the same sixteen teams in the same eleven cities. However, in March of 1953, the National League owners unanimously approved the Braves' move from Boston to Milwaukee. It was the first franchise shift in the National League since 1900. Since Milwaukee got a team, it gave hope to people in the Twin Cities.

John Cowles Sr., the owner of the *Minneapolis Star* and the *Minneapolis Tribune*, felt an area wasn't "big league" unless it had a major league baseball team. He and other civic leaders also knew that the Cities needed a new stadium before a team would move to Minnesota.

An independent group conducted a survey to determine where a stadium should be built. They came up with three choices: the first location was land adjacent to the state fairgrounds, the second was Bloomington, and the third was the Midway area of St. Paul. After a deal with the University of Minnesota to swap some land next to the fairgrounds unexpectedly fell through, attention turned to Bloomington.

Ground was broken for a new stadium near Cedar Avenue and Highway 100 in late June 1955. Less than a year later, Metropolitan Stadium was open for baseball. The Minneapolis

Millers, who had played at Nicollet Park since 1896, moved to Metropolitan Stadium and hosted the Wichita Braves in the inaugural game on April 24, 1956, with more than 18,000 in attendance.

While the Millers remained a popular attraction, the search continued for a big-league occupant for Met Stadium, and several teams flirted with the idea of moving to Minnesota in the early and mid-1950s. The St. Louis Browns and the Philadelphia Athletics were candidates to move and were rumored to be interested in the Twin Cities. (The Browns ended up moving to Baltimore and

In 1948, General Manager Rosy Ryan showed off the Millers to representatives of the New York Giants, including owner Horace Stoneham and former players Mel Ott and Carl Hubbell.

Calvin Griffith was president and principal owner of the Senators-Twins franchise for nearly thirty years.

became the Orioles in 1954; the Athletics relocated to Kansas City in 1955.)

The first franchise to seriously consider a move to the Twin Cities was the New York Giants, who had been the parent club of the Millers since 1946. In December 1948, the Giants purchased twenty acres of land near Highways 12 and 100 in St. Louis Park with the intention of building a new stadium for the Millers, but nothing ever came of those plans.

During the planning and construction of Metropolitan Stadium in 1955–56, the Giants had a say in the ballpark's design and how it would be expanded. The team's groundskeeper and assistant groundskeeper were in the Twin Cities for a month to help work on the field.

In May 1956, New York Giants owner Horace Stoneham furthered the rumors of a move when he was quoted in one of the New York papers as considering a move for the Giants from New York to Minneapolis. A delegation of some of the top civic leaders and businessmen in the Twin Cities went to New York. It seemed so certain that the Giants were going to move to Minneapolis, it didn't seem like anything would have to be negotiated.

The next thing we knew, the Giants announced they were moving to California following the 1957 season.

After that, the Twin Cities leaders began actively courting the Cleveland Indians. The Indians' fan attendance had sagged in the years following the team's American League pennant in 1954. One of the Indians' three majority owners was Ignatius O'Shaughnessy, a native of St. Paul. In the fall of 1957, the Indians' owners were all set to move the team to Minnesota. But the Indians' lease, which had been negotiated by Bill Veeck when he owned the team in the late 1940s, contained language that said the Indians could only play in Municipal Stadium. The Star and Tribune Company went to court to challenge the lease, but it was ironclad.

After the Giants, focus turned to the Washington Senators. In 1955 and 1956, the Senators had drawn barely more than 400,000 in attendance, the worst in the majors, and owner Calvin Griffith announced in late 1956 that he was considering moving his team unless it got a new stadium. Griffith said he had offers from Los Angeles, San Francisco, and Louisville, and the Twin Cities joined the competition to lure the Senators in 1958.

During the 1959 World Series, the *Sporting News* reported that Griffith was going to move the Senators to the Twin Cities for the following season. Griffith denied the report to the *Star and Tribune*, but he told the *Washington Post* that he was still open to the idea of moving and that he would review the Twin Cities' offer after the World Series.

The Twin Cities had offered Griffith a guaranteed annual attendance of 750,000 for the team's first five years in Minnesota. The Senators had drawn only 615,000 in 1959— the fifth straight year the team was at the bottom of the league in attendance—but Griffith turned down the offer. It didn't appear that the other American League owners would approve the move, so Calvin kept the team in Washington for 1960.

At about the same time that Minnesota began pursuing the Senators, a New York lawyer named William Shea announced he was going to start a third major league, to begin play in 1961. Known as the Continental League, it was to have eight teams representing the following cities: Minneapolis–St. Paul, Atlanta, Buffalo, Dallas, Denver,

The heart of the lineup during the team's first decade in Minnesota, Harmon "Killer" Killebrew slugged more home runs than any other player in Twins history.

By re-signing the young Bob Allison in 1961, Calvin Griffith locked up one of the team's cornerstone players of the next decade.

Houston, New York, and Toronto. Renowned baseball executive and former Dodgers general manager Branch Rickey would be president of the new league.

By early 1960, people in the Twin Cities started to give up on getting the Senators, and focus really turned to the Continental League. In January, Branch Rickey came to town and told a gathering that the Twin Cities were very important to the Continental League.

As Rickey and Shea worked to bolster support for the new league, the two existing major leagues took action. National League owners met in Chicago on July 18, 1960, and voted to expand from eight to ten teams. The American League owners followed suit shortly thereafter.

On August 2, the Continental League announced that it was folding. The American and National Leagues agreed to expand into cities that would have been part of the Continental League.

Both major leagues had an interest in placing a team in the Twin Cities, and that put Griffith in a bind. Calvin was still interested in moving his team to Minnesota, and he would lose that option if either league expanded to the Twin Cities. The Cities already had the advantage of a stadium that could be expanded for big-league use.

In mid-October, the National League announced that it would expand to Houston and New York. Finally, on October 26, the American League owners voted to allow the Senators to move to the Twin Cities in 1961 and become the Minnesota Twins. It would also expand by two teams—one in Los Angeles and a new team in Washington to replace the Senators.

Eight years of effort finally paid off for Minnesota.

Twins backstop Earl Battey won three consecutive Gold Glove Awards from 1960 to 1962.

A Pennant for the Cities: The Twins' First Decade

The Washington Senators were around for a quarter-century before reaching baseball's ultimate goal, the World Series. It took the franchise a mere five seasons to get there after moving to Minnesota. And after years of struggling to get fans to come to the ballpark in Washington, Calvin Griffith suddenly owned a ball club that drew over a million fans in each of the first ten seasons in Minnesota and led the American League (AL) in attendance over the Twins' first decade, from 1961 to 1970.

Despite averaging ninety-three losses over the final six seasons in Washington, the Senators started showing some promise by the start of the 1960s. They had young, up-and-coming sluggers like Harmon Killebrew and Bob Allison. Camilo Pascual was developing into a top starter, and lefty Jim Kaat was just getting his feet wet. After three consecutive last-place finishes, the team finished fifth in 1960 with a 73-81 record, its best since 1953. During their first season in Minnesota, the Twins dropped back to seventh place with a 70-90 record in 1961.

By 1962, the Twins were in the pennant race. They won ninety-one games that season and finished in second place, five games behind the first-place New York Yankees. Killebrew won the home run crown with forty-eight and also topped the league with 126 runs batted in. Pascual produced Minnesota's first twenty-game winner and led the American League in strikeouts.

The Twins came back with another 91-win campaign in 1963, but finished third and thirteen games behind the Yankees, who won 104 games. The team blasted a franchise-record 225 home runs in 1963 with Killebrew's league-high forty-five leading the way, followed by Bob Allison's thirty-five, and thirty-three more from rookie outfielder Jimmie Hall. Pascual was the AL strikeout king for the second year in a row and posted a record of 21-9.

They slipped to a 79-83 finish in 1964, but power remained the name of the Twins' game as the team banged out 221 homers. After the disappointing finish, Griffith made some changes to the coaching staff. He brought in Billy Martin as the third-base coach and Johnny Sain as the pitching coach.

While the team was getting plenty of slugging from Killebrew and others, Griffith wanted the team to run more. They stole a league-worst thirty-three bases as a team in 1962 (Los Angeles' Maury Wills stole 104 bases on his own

in 1962) and just thirty-two bases in 1963. The following year they amassed forty-six stolen bases, which was good enough for eighth-best in the league, but Martin and manager Sam Mele took it up a notch in 1965. The Twins doubled their production and stole ninety-two bases. The improvement was largely due to shortstop Zoilo Versalles, who stole twenty-seven bases in 1965 after stealing just fourteen in 1964.

Sam Mele took over the managerial reins early in the 1961 season and went on to skipper the Twins to the pennant in 1965.

As the pieces started falling into place on the field, the Twins had to overcome some turmoil in the clubhouse in 1965. Sain and Martin didn't get along, and Mele sided with Martin. Injuries also became an issue. Killebrew missed nearly fifty games, while Allison missed twenty-seven games and battled a slump. Camilo Pascual, who won fifteen games for the Twins in 1964, missed over a month in 1965 and won just nine games. Jim "Mudcat" Grant and Jim Kaat picked up the slack by winning twenty-one and eighteen games, respectively.

One moment from the 1965 season really stands out. On the final weekend before the All-Star Game—which was being played at Metropolitan Stadium—the five-time-defending American League champion New York Yankees came to town for a three-game series. On Sunday afternoon, in the final game of the series, the Twins were down by two runs going into the bottom of the ninth. They rallied to put two runners on, and Killebrew knocked a three-run home run off pitcher Pete Mikkelsen to win the game. The Twins headed into the All-Star break atop the standings by a full five games—a lead they would not relinquish.

Two days after the conclusion of that dramatic series against the Yankees, fourteen future Hall of Famers graced the Metropolitan Stadium field for the annual midsummer classic. The National League fielded one of the greatest teams ever at that All-Star Game, including eleven future Hall of Famers, plus Pete Rose, the all-time hits leader, and Joe Torre, who might make the Hall of Fame as a manager. Killebrew hit a home run in the game, but the National League won 6-5.

The Twins went on to win 102 games that year and captured the 1965 American League pennant. They played the Los Angeles Dodgers of Sandy Koufax and Don Drysdale in the World Series. Minnesota won the first two games at Met Stadium behind complete-game victories by Grant and Kaat. The Dodgers then took the next three games in Los Angeles to take a three-games-to-two lead. The series returned to Minnesota, and the Twins won Game Six— Grant pitched another complete game and hit a home run—to tie the series. In the deciding seventh game, Koufax was pitching on just two days' rest, but he was practically unhittable. He led the Dodgers to a 2-0 victory.

Righty Jim "Mudcat" Grant and lefty Jim Kaat combined to win 105 games for the Twins between 1964 and 1966.

Bob Allison connects for one of his thirty-two home runs in 1964. He averaged thirty homers during the team's first five seasons in Minnesota.

Another young star for the Twins in the early 1960s, Zoilo Versalles won the American League MVP Award in 1965.

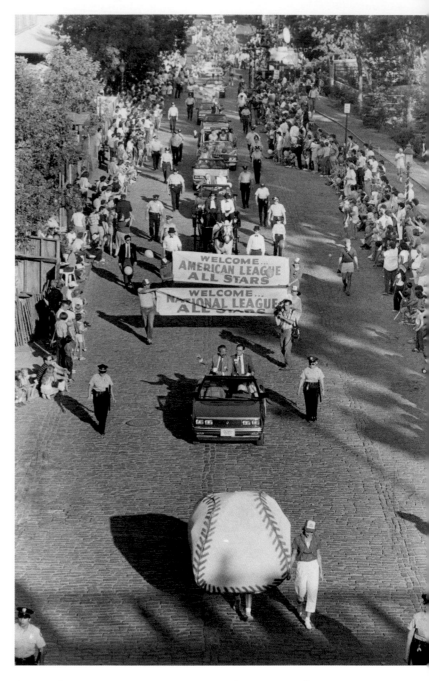

St. Paul Mayor George Latimer and Minneapolis Mayor Don Fraser led the parade to welcome the Major League All-Star Game in July 1965.

The Twins might have won Game Seven were it not for a great fielding play by Dodgers third baseman Junior Gilliam in the fifth inning. Trailing 2-0, the Twins had runners at first and second with one out when Versalles hit a hard grounder down the line. Gilliam snared it and forced out the runner at third. Koufax, who allowed just three hits on the day, got out of the inning and shut them out the rest of the way.

The 1965 fall classic really put the Twin Cities on the sports map. The World Series was the biggest thing in sports at the time. The NFL was just starting to grow, and there was

no Super Bowl yet. The NBA was nothing like it is today. The NHL was made up of just six teams, two of them in Canada, and it didn't get national coverage.

The Twins nearly returned to the World Series in 1967. Heading into the final weekend of the season, the Twins were sitting in first place. They were one game ahead of the

The 1965 All-Star Game drew a capacity crowd to Metropolitan Stadium.

Boston Red Sox and Detroit Tigers. They went into Boston's Fenway Park for a two-game series, and they needed to win just one game to clinch the pennant. Jim Kaat started the first game and was leading 1-0 in the bottom of the third when he felt something pop in his arm and had to leave the game. The Red Sox came back to win, 6-4, and they won the next day, 5-3, to grab the pennant.

The Twins and Tigers each finished with ninety-one wins to end in a tie for second place, one game behind Boston. Boston's top star that year was Carl Yastrzemski, who had played for the Minneapolis Millers in 1959 and 1960 before heading to the majors. Yastrzemski had the best season of his career in 1967, winning the Triple Crown by leading the American League in homers (44), runs batted in (121), and batting average (.326).

Cal Ermer, who took over as the Twins manager fifty games into the 1967 season, led the team to a disappointing seventh-place finish in 1968. In 1969, Calvin Griffith handed the reins to their fiery third-base coach, Billy Martin.

Metropolitan Stadium hosted a World Series in just its fifth season of major league use.

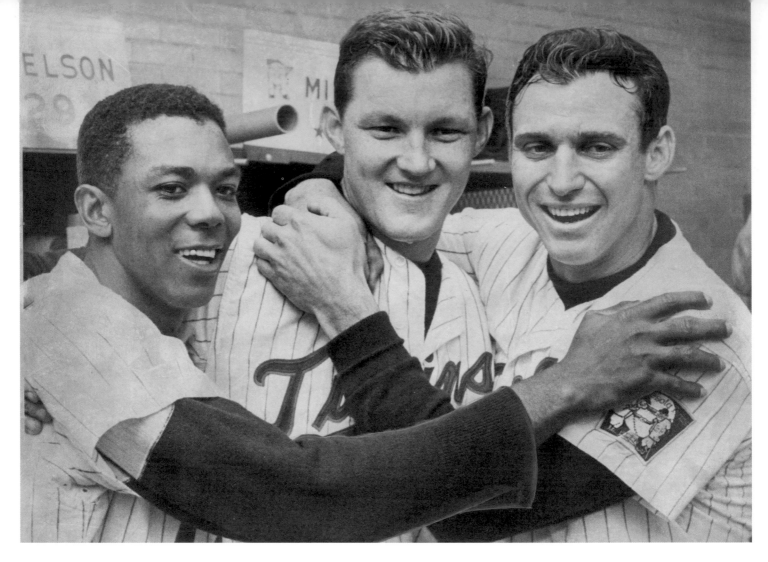

Tony Oliva, Jim Kaat, and Bob Allison celebrate after Minnesota won Game Two of the 1965 World Series.

The Twins finished with ninety-seven victories in 1969 to win the American League West Division. Killebrew smacked forty-nine homers and drove in 140 runs en route to winning the Most Valuable Player Award, and Minnesota's twenty-three-year-old second baseman, Rod Carew, won his first career batting title with a .332 mark. On the mound, the Twins had a pair of twenty-game winners in Dave Boswell and Jim Perry.

The Twins lost the first two games of the American League Championship Series in Baltimore—both by one run—and Griffith urged Martin to start Kaat in Game Three. But Martin sent Bob Miller to the mound, and he only lasted into the second inning. The Orioles won the game, 11-2, and wrapped up the three-game sweep.

Griffith fired Martin after one season as manager—it was one of the biggest mistakes Griffith ever made.

During the season, Martin had been involved in a fight with one of his players (Boswell) in a bar in Detroit, but

Pitcher Jim Grant leaps home after blasting a three-run homer in Game Six. He also pitched a complete game.

A dejected fan mourns the Twins' loss in the final game of the 1965 series.

Griffith had been in his corner up to this point. Griffith's brothers—team executives Jimmy and Billy Robertson—also were big supporters of Martin.

But Griffith listened to Howard Fox, his traveling secretary, who convinced him to fire Martin. It was an injustice.

Billy Martin was by far the most popular manager the Twins have ever had. Tom Kelly won two World Series, but Billy would have owned this town.

A typical scene from Billy Martin's tenure as the Twins' manager. Here he argues with umpire Bill Kunkel during a game against Cleveland in June 1969.

Rod Carew

One of Calvin Griffith's greatest assets as a team owner was his farm system and scouting department.

In June of 1964, Twins scout Herb Stein—who scouted for Griffith for forty years—discovered Rod Carew on a sandlot in New York City. The Twins signed the eighteen-year-old Carew as a free agent, and he spent three years in the Twins' minor-league system.

In 1967, Griffith ordered Twins manager Sam Mele to make Carew the Twins' second baseman. Carew got off to a slow start, and some people in the organization wanted Carew sent back to the minors because they didn't think he was ready. But Griffith told Mele to stick with the young infielder. Carew went on to be the Twins starting second baseman for the next nine years, before switching to first base in 1976.

Rod Carew was the team's top hitter in every season from 1972 to 1977.

Carew had a fantastic season in 1977. He flirted with .400 for much of the year and ended up hitting .388—the highest batting average in the major leagues in twenty years, since Ted Williams hit .388 for the Boston Red Sox in 1957. It was Carew's sixth American League batting title, and he earned the league's Most Valuable Player Award. Griffith gave Carew a $100,000 bonus following the season.

A threat on the base paths as well as at the plate, Carew stole home seventeen times in his career.

Carew won another batting title in 1978, but it became evident that Griffith wasn't going to be able to pay Carew the salary he deserved. In February 1979, Griffith traded Carew to the California Angels for four players: Ken Landreaux, Dave Engle, Paul Hartzell, and Brad Havens.

Carew played seven seasons for the Angels before retiring in 1985. He retired with more than 3,000 hits and a .328 career batting average. Rod Carew was inducted into the National Baseball Hall of Fame in 1991 in his first year of eligibility.

On Top of the World:
Two Twins Championships

Without question, the Twins' world titles in 1987 and 1991 mark the pinnacle of baseball in Minnesota, and perhaps all of Minnesota professional sports. The two championships energized the Twin Cities sports scene like never before. But it was a rough ride getting there.

After coming up short in 1967 and 1969, the Twins faced some tough times in the 1970s. Firing Martin hurt their attendance. After drawing 1.35 million in 1969 and 1.26 million in 1970, when they won another West Division title, the team drew over a million fans only

A young Rod Carew swings for the fences during a game against Oakland in 1968. Carew provided the rare bright spot for the Twins in the early 1970s.

Kirby Puckett and Kent Hrbek were the heart and soul of the Twins for more than a decade. Here Puckett offers congratulations after one of Hrbek's twenty-nine homers in 1986.

Gene Mauch

Calvin Griffith hired Gene Mauch to be the Twins manager in 1976. The Twins finished that season 85-77, just five games behind the division-champion Kansas City Royals, and Mauch might have had a good chance to win the division if only Griffith had found him a pitcher.

Mauch got his start as a manager with the Minneapolis Millers in 1958 and 1959. He led them to back-to-back appearances in the Junior World Series.

It was around this time that I had a conversation with John Quinn, the general manager of the Philadelphia Phillies, whom I had gotten to know really well when he ran the Milwaukee Braves. Late in spring training of 1960, Quinn called me and said, "What do you know about Mauch?" I replied, "What do you want to know about him?"

Quinn asked me if Mauch could get along with the press and what kind of manager he was. I told him he'd get along with the press and that on a scale of one to ten, "He's a ten." Quinn said, "Okay, you've got a scoop tomorrow. Don't quote me, but just say rumors are that Gene Mauch is going to be the Phillies manager."

The Phillies lost their season opener in 1960 and fired manager Eddie Sawyer. Gene Mauch became the new manager.

Mauch led the Phillies to within one game of the pennant in 1964, but fell short in a heartbreaking season for Philadelphia. He later won division titles with the California Angels in 1982 and 1986, but again failed to make it to the World Series. With 1,902 career victories in his twenty-six-year managerial career, Mauch is the winningest manager in major league history to never reach the World Series.

Despite this disappointment, Mauch was a great, great manager. I think, from a baseball standpoint, he was as good as ever lived. Rod Carew said that Mauch was the best manager he ever played for. Mauch was loved.

Gene Mauch led the Twins to three winning seasons in five years, but he never got them to the postseason.

two more times (1977 and 1979) for the remainder of the decade.

The arrival of free agency in the mid-1970s severely hampered the Twins' ability to compete. Calvin Griffith had been one of the smartest operators in the game, and as long as he was working on equal financial footing, few club owners could compete with him. Yet, free agency made it nearly impossible for Griffith to retain his best players and he didn't have the money to sign free agents. Newspaper writers all over the country ripped Griffith.

The Twins had strong teams in 1976 and 1977 under manager Gene Mauch, and they had a shot at a division

Third baseman Gary Gaetti won four Gold Glove Awards and pounded 201 homers in nine seasons as a Twin.

Tom Brunansky (center) was Minnesota's representative at the 1985 All-Star Game at the Metrodome.

Tom Kelly was one of only three people to manage two championship teams between 1985 and 2005.

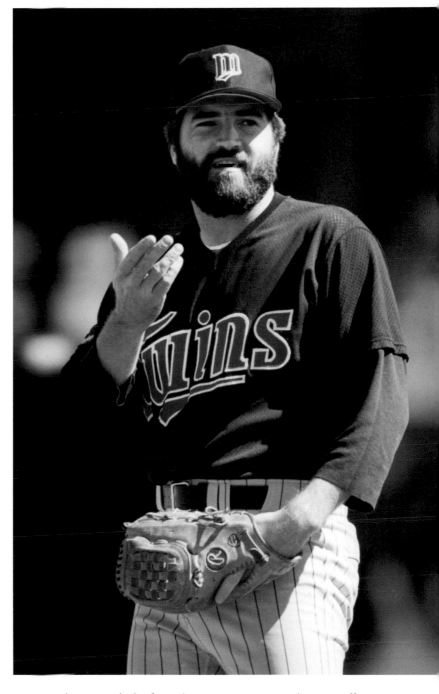

Acquired in a trade before the 1987 season, reliever Jeff Reardon led the Twins with thirty-one saves that year.

title. With Rod Carew at first base and an outfield of Larry Hisle, Danny Ford, and Lyman Bostock, they had some guys that could hit the ball. They called that team "the lumber company." But after not re-signing Hisle or pitcher Bill Campbell and trading away Bert Blyleven midway through the 1976 season, the team began a downward slide.

Kent Hrbek

In June 1978, the Minnesota Twins selected Kent Hrbek in the seventeenth round of the Amateur Draft.

The Twins offered Hrbek, who grew up near Metropolitan Stadium in Bloomington, a $5,000 bonus. Hrbek had a scholarship offer to play for the Gophers, and so he turned down the bonus from the Twins and started playing for the American Legion team in Bloomington.

Twins scout Angelo Giuliani really liked Hrbek, who was big and could hit for power. Giuliani convinced Calvin Griffith to go and watch Hrbek play in a Legion game. Hrbek hit a tape-measure home run, and Griffith decided to sign him for a $30,000 bonus.

Hrbek turned out to be a bargain. He spent just a little over two seasons in the minors and went from Class A to the big leagues in August of 1981. Twins vice president Bruce Haynes convinced Griffith to recall Hrbek from Visalia of the California League, even though he was only twenty-one.

He hit a homer in his first major-league game, in the twelfth inning, to lift the Twins to a 3-2 victory over the Yankees.

His recall to the majors was the start of building the 1987 championship team. Gary Gaetti was recalled in September of 1981, and he also hit a home run in his first game.

Hrbek was central to the Twins' two World Series teams before retiring after the 1994 season at the age of thirty-four. During his thirteen-year career, Hrbek hit twenty or more home runs in ten seasons, and he retired in second place, behind Harmon Killebrew, on the franchise's all-time career home run list with 293.

Known mostly for his bat, first baseman Hrbek was also stellar with the glove.

Kent Hrbek hit 293 regular-season home runs in his career, but few were bigger than this grand slam in Game Six of the 1987 World Series.

Hrbek celebrates the final out that clinched the pennant against the Detroit Tigers in the 1987 American League Championship Series (ALCS).

Attendance began to climb again after the Twins' new stadium—the Hubert H. Humphrey Metrodome—opened in 1982, but the team failed to finish above .500 in the first five years at the Dome. Griffith felt he couldn't afford the big contracts of players like shortstop Roy Smalley, catcher Butch Wynegar, and pitcher Doug Corbett, and he decided to rebuild with younger players who mostly earned the minimum salary. Fortunately, among the young players on that 1982 team were Kent Hrbek, Gary Gaetti, Tom Brunansky, Frank Viola, and others who would be key pieces of the team that would reach the World Series just five years later.

The 1987 World Series was the first one ever played in a dome. The Twins packed in more than 55,000 fans in each of the four games.

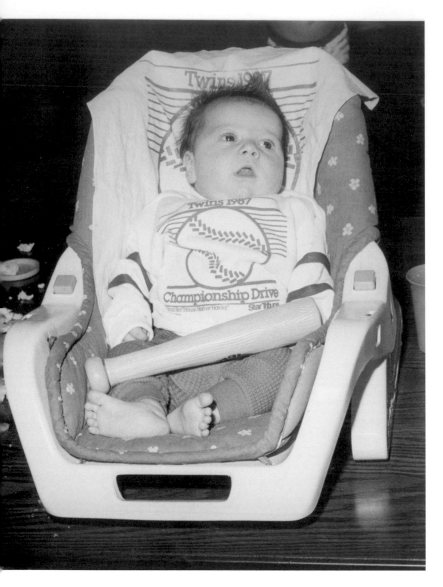

Twins fans of all ages got into the act to cheer on the team during the 1987 championship run.

Back for his second stint with the Twins, Bert Blyleven started and got the win in Game Two of the 1987 series.

In 1983, Griffith failed to sign all three of the Twins' top draft picks (Tim Belcher, Bill Swift, and Oddibe McDowell). It was becoming increasingly clear that he didn't have the money to continue owning the team. He was ready to sell to a group in Tampa Bay, and if the Twins didn't sell 1.8 million tickets in a season, he could get out of the Metrodome lease. Minneapolis' Harvey Mackay raised $6 million to buy up the tickets, until Griffith started looking for local buyers.

There is no doubt that Griffith would have moved the team, but the league didn't want to leave this market, which is the fourteenth largest in the country.

In 1984, Minneapolis banker Carl Pohlad bought the team from Griffith for $36 million. It was a sad day for the Griffith family; they had owned the franchise for seventy-two years.

Pohlad was a savior. He stepped in and bought the team when there was a good chance it would move if a local buyer wasn't found.

After two more losing seasons in 1985 and 1986, the Twins improved to 85-77 in 1987. Despite a regular-season record

Minnesota Twins are World Champions!

Pitcher Frank Viola gets a hug from pitching coach Dick Such after Game Seven. Viola was the 1987 World Series MVP.

that was only ninth-best among the twenty-six major league teams, the Twins won the American League West Division by two games over the Kansas City Royals. They were back in the postseason for the first time in seventeen years.

The Twins had two good starting pitchers in Frank Viola and Bert Blyleven—the latter back for a second stint with the team after being re-acquired from the Indians in 1985—and two good relievers in Jeff Reardon and Juan Berenguer. They also had four batters who hit twenty-eight or more home runs: Kent Hrbek (34), Tom Brunansky (32), Gary Gaetti (31), and Kirby Puckett (28).

Nobody gave the Twins much of a chance in the postseason, but in the American League playoffs and the World Series, the Twins showed they could play with the best.

In the American League Championship Series (ALCS), they were matched up against the Detroit Tigers, who posted

Puckett gets a champagne shower after carrying the Twins to victory in the 1991 American League Championship Series.

Greg Gagne's three-run homer helped to secure the victory in Game One of the 1991 World Series. He is congratulated by Dan Gladden and Kent Hrbek (14).

the best record in baseball that year (98-64). The Tigers had Alan Trammell, Kirk Gibson, Darrell Evans, and St. Paul native Jack Morris.

The Metrodome gave the Twins a big home-field advantage during the regular season—they were 56-25 at home but only 29-52 on the road—and the ALCS was scheduled to open in Minnesota. True to form, the Twins won the first two games at the Dome. In Game Two they beat Morris, who had a record of 11-0 against the Twins in Minnesota prior to that game.

The Tigers won Game Three in Detroit, but the Twins won Game Four behind Viola, and then wrapped up the pennant with a 9-5 victory in Game Five. Despite their poor regular-season road record, the Twins had clinched the division title on the road, at Texas, and won the ALCS by taking two of three games in Detroit.

The Twins went on to play the St. Louis Cardinals in the World Series, which also opened in Minnesota. They won the first two games at the Metrodome—the first World Series games ever played in a domed stadium—but the

The 1991 series was full of drama. Here, Dan Gladden upends Atlanta catcher Greg Olson while trying to score in Game One.

Kirby Puckett told his teammates to climb on his back during the 1991 World Series, and he came through again and again. His leaping catch to rob Atlanta's Ron Gant of a hit helped save Game Six for the Twins.

Puckett's eleventh-inning blast in Game Six set the stage for an epic seventh game.

Cardinals won the next three games in St. Louis. The Twins won Games Six and Seven at the Metrodome.

Commissioner Peter Ueberroth said that when he became commissioner in 1984 a lot of people had told him the Twin Cities shouldn't have a baseball franchise. After attending the World Series in Minnesota, he called the Twins fans the best baseball fans he had ever seen.

In 1988, the Twins became the first American League team to break three million in attendance for a season. Viola went 24-7 and earned the Cy Young Award. The Twins won ninety-one games, but finished thirteen games behind the division-winning Oakland A's. It was the first of three consecutive American League titles for Oakland.

Kirby Puckett

Kirby Puckett was the most popular athlete in Minnesota history.

On the field, Puckett was unquestionably a superstar. He was the first major-league baseball player to sign a contract worth $3 million a year. At the time of his retirement in 1996, he was earning $6 million a year—but the money never changed him.

Although his on-the-field accomplishments set Puckett apart as one of the game's best, it was his hustle, enthusiasm, and playfulness that earned the respect and admiration of fans, teammates, and opposing players alike. Chicago Cubs president Andy MacPhail, who was the Twins general manager during their championship seasons in 1987 and 1991, called Puckett "the best teammate" he's ever seen.

With a short and stocky build and originally from the projects of Chicago, Puckett didn't exactly have all the ingredients for a professional baseball career. Fortunately, he was discovered by Twins assistant farm director Jim Rantz.

In the summer of 1981, Major League Baseball was on strike and Rantz went to Peoria, Illinois, to watch his son play in a summer college league. During the first game, Rantz saw a stocky outfielder named Kirby Puckett hit a double, triple, and a home run, steal a couple of bases, throw out a base runner at home, and make a couple of good catches in centerfield. Rantz really liked Puckett's hustle—he was the first player on and off the field—and his personality, as well as his skills.

That fall Puckett enrolled at Triton Junior College in River Grove, Illinois. In January 1982, on Rantz's recommendation, the Twins selected Puckett with the third pick in the secondary phase draft. Most major league scouts considered the five-foot-eight-inch Puckett too short to play in the big leagues.

The Twins offered Puckett $5,000, but he turned it down and remained in River Grove. The Twins held the rights to Puckett until June, and he would have gone back into the draft if they didn't sign him. Puckett hit .400 at Triton that season and led the team to the Junior College World Series. The Twins signed Puckett for a $25,000 bonus.

During his first year in pro ball, Puckett batted .382 for Elizabethton in the rookie league. He played a little over two years in the minors before being called up by the Twins in May of 1984.

More than just a Hall of Fame player, Kirby Puckett was the most beloved athlete in Minnesota sports history.

Puckett was a hit right away with the Twins. He had four hits in his major-league debut against the Angels in Anaheim. He collected 2,040 hits in his first ten seasons in the majors. Only one other major leaguer—Willie Keeler with 2,065—had more hits in his first ten years.

Late in the 1995 season, Puckett was hit in the face with a pitch by Cleveland's Dennis Martinez. He reported to camp in the spring of 1996 in good shape and was having a great spring training until an eye problem surfaced less than a week before the regular-season opener. Puckett opened the 1996 season on the disabled list—the first time in his career he had been on the injured list—and following several surgeries he was forced to retire.

After retiring as a player, Puckett served as the Twins executive vice president for baseball until December of 2002. The Twins and Puckett had discussions about him staying with the team in some capacity, but they couldn't reach an agreement. Personal issues led Puckett to drop further out of the public eye over the last few years of his life.

Puckett, a ten-time all-star and six-time Gold Glove Award winner, was elected to the Hall of Fame in 2001 during his first year of eligibility. His .318 career average is fifth best in franchise history, and second only to Carew since the team came to Minnesota.

At the time of his retirement, Kirby Puckett was one of the most popular players in the big leagues and the most popular athlete in Minnesota history. In December 1999, the *Star Tribune* named him number one on the list of the one hundred most influential Minnesota sports figures of the twentieth century.

Kirby Puckett died from a stroke on March 6, 2006, eight days before his forty-sixth birthday.

Ever since he burst on the scene in 1984, Puckett always seemed to have a smile on his face.

Puckett's playful attitude and easy-going nature made him popular with teammates and opponents alike.

Kirby Puckett always had plenty of reasons to celebrate.

Jack Morris' ten-inning shutout in the final game of the 1991 World Series was one of the best pitching performances in postseason history.

second baseman Chuck Knoblauch brought speed at the top of the order. The Twins also signed pitcher and hometown boy Jack Morris, while youngsters Kevin Tapani and Scott Erickson bolstered the starting rotation. Rick Aguilera keyed the bullpen with his forty-two saves during the regular season. The Twins won 95 games to win the division by eight games over the Chicago White Sox. In the playoffs, the Twins beat the Blue Jays four games to one in the ALCS. The Twins met the Atlanta Braves, who had also finished last in the previous season, in the 1991 World Series.

The 1991 World Series was one of the greatest ever played. Five of the seven games were decided by a single run, and four of them in the final at bat.

The Twins won the first two games in the Metrodome, but the Braves won the next three in Atlanta including a 14-5 romp in Game Five.

The series returned to Minneapolis and the Twins won Game Six in dramatic fashion, behind Puckett's game-winning blast in the eleventh inning. Game Seven was a true gem. Morris went the distance in a ten-inning, 1-0 shutout victory to bring another championship banner to Minnesota. I've watched a lot of great athletes over the years, but I've never seen a competitor like Morris.

The 1991 team was the best of the Twins' three World Series teams. The 1991 club had more depth, better pitching, and more talented athletes than the 1965 and 1987 teams. The 1965 and 1987 teams had more power, but the starting pitching for the 1991 team was as good as the 1965 team and the relief pitching was even better.

Although the two teams featured some different faces, the Twins of 1987 and 1991 are in rare company among teams of the free-agent era. Between 1980 and 2005, only two other ball clubs—the Toronto Blue Jays of 1992–93 and the New York Yankees of 1996–2000—were able to win more than one world championship in a five-year span. Tom Kelly's bunch accomplished the feat with a combination of homegrown talent and some key free-agent acquisitions.

In 1990, the Twins finished last in the AL West with a 74-88 record. But they rebounded in 1991.

In 1991, the Twins no longer had Brunansky, Gaetti, or Viola, but they still had Puckett and Hrbek. They added power and veteran leadership in designated hitter Chili Davis, whom they signed in the off-season, and rookie

Rising from the Ashes

If the Twins of 1987 and 1991 marked the apex of Minnesota baseball, the period from 1993 to 2000 was a low point. Just when it looked like things were starting to turn around, the specter of contraction appeared and threatened to kill off the franchise once and for all. Through these challenges, however, the Twins emerged as one of the best young teams in the league and posted three consecutive ninety-win seasons for the first time in franchise history.

Following the 1991 title, the Twins seemed poised to win another pennant in 1992. In fact, many people thought that team was going to be the best one of all. In spring training, the Twins traded for pitcher John Smiley, who had won twenty games for Pittsburgh in 1991. Smiley won sixteen games in 1992, and the Twins won ninety, but they fell short and finished six games behind Oakland.

It went downhill quickly for the Twins after 1992. The team dropped to sixth place in 1993, which was the start of eight consecutive losing seasons. They had the worst record in baseball between 1993 and 1997 and failed to finish higher than fourth place in the five-team Central Division from 1994 to 2000. In 1996, the Twins' ten-time all-star Kirby Puckett was forced to retire at the age of thirty-six because of eye problems. Nothing seemed to be going right for the Twins.

Commissioner Bud Selig's announcement that Major League Baseball might contract the team shocked the Twins community.

Twins fans rallied at the Metrodome to support the team and fight the contraction plans in 2002.

Brad Radke, who stuck with the Twins through tough times in the late 1990s, has been the team's ace righty for more than a decade.

In 2001, during Tom Kelly's final season as the Twins' manager, the team finally climbed above .500, going 85-77 and finishing second in the division. The team had some talented young players and most had come up through the Twins minor league system. Things were starting to look brighter for Minnesota baseball.

In November of 2001, two days after the World Series ended, Commissioner Bud Selig announced that Major League Baseball was planning to eliminate two franchises. The teams that were originally targeted for contraction were the Florida Marlins and the Montreal Expos. Then, owner Carl Pohlad offered the Twins for contraction.

The Twins had made money from an operating standpoint in 2000 and 2001, but it was not enough to pay the interest on the $90 million loan Pohlad took out when he bought the club in 1984. Pohlad was tired of losing money and tired of the ongoing stadium debates. So he decided to accept the contraction buyout for a price reportedly between $150 and $200 million. Including the $36 million he paid for the team in 1984, Pohlad had about $150 million invested in the team.

Before baseball could go through with contracting the Twins, a Hennepin County district court judge issued an injunction saying that the team had to honor its lease to play in the Metrodome in 2002. I think Major League Baseball also realized it was going to have legal problems with contraction. In addition to the Hennepin County judge, the Major League Baseball Players Association was going to fight contraction over the loss of jobs that would result.

Through all the distractions, the Minnesota Twins won the American League Central Division crown in 2002 and returned to the playoffs for the first since 1991. The Twins surprised some people by beating the Oakland A's in five games in the first round of the playoffs. Minnesota won the series opener in Oakland, but then fell behind two games to one. They bounced back to win the final two games and held on for a 5-4 victory in Game Five in Oakland.

The Twins won the opening game of the ALCS in Anaheim, but the Angels won the next four games to advance to the World Series.

The 2002 crown was the first of three consecutive division titles for the Twins. They won 90 or more games in all three seasons, but they were matched up against powerful Yankees teams in the American League Division Series in 2003 and again in 2004. They lost in both years three games to one.

Leaping, home-run-robbing catches have been a familiar sight for as long as Torii Hunter has been roaming center field.

Left-fielder Shannon Stewart gets into the act with this spectacular grab at Yankee Stadium during the 2003 Division Series against New York.

Torii Hunter and the Twins celebrated their third consecutive division title in 2004.

In 2005, the Central Division got a lot tougher, seemingly overnight. The Chicago White Sox became one of the better teams in baseball by adding several key players, including former Twin A.J. Pierzynski. Cleveland was also much improved and won ninety-three games to finish six games behind the division-winning White Sox. Although the Twins' 83-79 record marked their fifth-consecutive winning season—the first time in franchise history that had happened—the team finished third in the division and missed the postseason. The White Sox, of course, went on to win the World Series, their first title in eighty-eight years.

What really helped the Twins' turnaround was their farm system. General manager Terry Ryan and Jim Rantz, director of the Twins minor leagues, have done a great job. The Minnesota Twins were named organization of the year in 2000 by Topps, and again in 2002 by *Baseball America*. Ryan was named major league executive of the year in 2002 by *The Sporting News* and in 2004 by *Baseball America*. Rantz doesn't get enough credit for the job he does.

Of all the players brought in by Ryan and the Twins, none had more to do with the team's turnaround than pitcher Johan Santana. In 2004 and 2005, Santana was the

No pitcher was as dominating as Johan Santana in 2004 and 2005.

St. Paul's own Joe Mauer was selected by the Twins with the first overall pick in the 2001 amateur draft.

most dominant pitcher I've seen since Sandy Koufax in the mid 1960s. In 2004, Santana was virtually untouchable after the All-Star break. He allowed just 55 hits and 14 earned runs in 104 innings. He went 13-0—the thirteen consecutive victories were a team record—with a 1.21 earned run average (ERA) in the second half of the season. For the year, opponents batted just .192 against him. He finished with a 20-6 record and 2.61 ERA; he was good enough to win the Cy Young Award—joining Frank Viola and Jim Perry as the only Twins to win it.

In 2005, Santana pitched nearly as well as he had in 2004, but he didn't get the run support as the Twins offense struggled. For the season, he was 16-7 with a 2.87 ERA, and he led the entire major leagues in strikeouts.

Simply put, Johan Santana has become one of the best pitchers in baseball.

The Stadium Debates

Stadium debates have been going on in Minnesota for more than fifty years.

In the 1950s, while the Twin Cities were pursuing a major league baseball or pro football franchise, two new baseball stadiums were built.

In November of 1953, voters in St. Paul passed a city-bond issue, which included $2 million to build Midway Stadium. The city of St. Paul hoped that Midway Stadium would eventually house a major league team.

Nine months later, a commission backed by the cities of Minneapolis, Bloomington, and Richfield also picked a site for a baseball stadium: Cedar Avenue and Highway 100 (the Beltline) in Bloomington. The commission paid about $500,000 for 164 acres. A group called the Minneapolis Minutemen led the bond drive to raise money for the stadium project.

In early June of 1955, the city of St. Paul broke ground for the new Midway Stadium. Later that month, ground was also broke in Bloomington for Metropolitan Stadium.

Construction of Metropolitan Stadium began in Bloomington in 1955 with hopes of someday hosting a major league occupant.

The Hubert H. Humphrey Metrodome opened in 1982 to mixed reviews.

By the early 1970s, talk started up about building a new stadium for the Minnesota Vikings and Minnesota Twins, since both teams' leases were set to expire in 1975. Some people in Minneapolis thought this was a chance to build a stadium downtown. The debate got pretty heated.

Senator Hubert Humphrey was in favor of a new stadium. In a talk to the Minnesota House DFL Caucus in March of 1976, Humphrey said, "Great sports events are good for this community and are the best way to make Minnesota known to the rest of the country. Without professional sports, the Twin Cities would be just a cold Omaha. Don't miss the chance to give this state an opportunity to move forward."

A stadium bill was finally passed during the 1977 legislative session on the third try. Construction started on the Hubert H. Humphrey Metrodome in December 1979.

The Metrodome opened in 1982, and by the mid 1990s, the Twins started talking about a new stadium again. A decade later, the Twins are still trying to get a new stadium.

It's hard to understand how other cities can build successful new stadiums, and this area is still opposed to the idea.

The Metrodome is one of the oldest stadiums in the American League, after Boston, New York, Oakland, and Kansas City. The Yankees are getting a new stadium, scheduled to open in 2009. Eighteen new major league baseball stadiums have opened since 1990, and New York and Washington will have new ballparks within the next three years; another ballpark in Anaheim was completely remodeled.

Over this same period, seventeen new stadiums have opened in the NFL. Some cities—including Baltimore, Cincinnati, Cleveland, Denver, Detroit, Houston, and Seattle, among others—have built two new stadiums. Pennsylvania Governor Tom Ridge made sure that Pittsburgh and Philadelphia had stadiums for both their football and baseball teams.

Our governor hasn't provided any leadership here. There don't seem to be politicians like Governor Rudy Perpich, Governor Arne Carlson, or Senator Hubert Humphrey around to back a new stadium. I think the real reason the stadium issues haven't been resolved is private leadership. When the Twin Cities were pursuing major league sports in the 1950s, civic leaders like John Cowles Sr. and Donald Dayton put their money where their mouths were. We don't have leaders like that now.

Back then, companies like General Mills, Pillsbury, and Dayton's really helped the local situation. You don't have that today.

Carl Pohlad has gotten a lot of heat during the stadium debates of the last few years. Since he's a billionaire, many people feel that he should build his own stadium. But that hasn't happened in other cities. I think people still hold a grudge over the 1997 deal.

In January of 1997, Governor Carlson and Pohlad announced that they had a deal by which the Twins would contribute $90 million toward construction of a $350 million stadium, and the state would get a minority interest in the team as part of a public-ownership plan. About a month

By 1985, more than a million fans were coming to the Dome to watch the Twins every year.

Carl Pohlad has been at the center of the stadium debates ever since he became the team owner in 1984.

later, the Twins held a press conference to show off a model for the proposed stadium.

The news conference where the deal was first announced just confused everybody. It wasn't explained what Pohlad would contribute to the stadium and what he would get in return. People thought Pohlad was giving money to the state, but it turned out that it was just a loan. Right away people started to criticize the deal.

By late August of 1997, Pohlad was keeping a low profile about the stadium issue and the fate of the Twins. The team had asked Major League Baseball for permission to look into moving to another city if a stadium wasn't built in the Twin Cities. Pohlad started getting offers from several cities to buy the team, including groups from North Carolina, Las Vegas, and Northern Virginia.

About this time, Pohlad got a visit from a North Carolina businessman named Don Beaver. Beaver, who was worth a reported $250 million, owned several minor league teams, including a Triple-A team in Charlotte, and he owned ten percent of the Pittsburgh Pirates.

In early October, Pohlad announced that he had an offer in writing from Beaver to buy the Twins for $150 million. Beaver wanted to move the team to the North Carolina Triad region (Greensboro, High Point, and Winston-Salem). The agreement between Pohlad and Beaver had a deadline of March 31, 1998, for signing the letter of intent to sell the team.

The agreement deadline passed without the deal getting signed as Pohlad and Beaver continued to negotiate. In May of 1998, voters in North Carolina went to the polls and voted against building a new stadium.

So, the deal never happened. A lot of people thought the Beaver-Pohlad deal was just a bluff designed to force the hand of the Twin Cities, but I thought it was more serious than that. I believe that the Charlotte group—which included Hugh McColl, the chief executive of NationsBank and a friend of Pohlad's—was legitimately interested, but Atlanta Braves owner Ted Turner killed any chance of the team moving to Charlotte. He didn't want another team that close to Atlanta. Turner was fighting it, and finally Major League Baseball decided the Charlotte market was too small.

In November of 1997, the Minnesota House of Representative held a special legislative session and voted 84-47 against a stadium deal.

So at the start of the 1998 season, the outlook for keeping the Twins here seemed dim. The team had sold less than 5,000 season tickets for 1998 and interest in the team was way down. In May, Pohlad said he would have no choice but to move the team if he didn't get some relief.

In March of 1999, St. Paul Mayor Norm Coleman decided to go after the Twins and put together a proposal to build a stadium in St. Paul. That November, the citizens of St. Paul voted down Coleman's initiative to impose a half-percent sales tax increase to pay for St. Paul's stake in a new Twins ballpark. The vote was 58 to 42 percent.

Pohlad had reached a tentative agreement to sell the team to Glen Taylor and Robert Naegele Jr. if St. Paul passed the initiative. The vote meant the deal was dead, and it left Pohlad uncertain about the team's future in Minnesota.

As early as the fall of 2000, the state legislature learned that contraction by Major League Baseball was a possibility. The legislature knew that if a stadium wasn't built, the Twins would be gone. Since the threat to move the team to North Carolina looked like a bluff, legislators didn't believe Baseball Commissioner Bud Selig.

In early 2001, Pohlad made a great offer of $150 million to help build a new stadium, but time had run out on the legislature. Although they had formed a committee to study the stadium issue, nothing was accomplished.

The 2001 baseball season was the Twins' first winning season since 1992, and the team had some talented young players who were going to be good. The future started looking a little brighter.

After eight years of effort, the legislature finally passed a Twins stadium bill in May 2002. But the bill was flawed. Instead of allowing two bodies—like Hennepin County and the city of Minneapolis—to partner on a stadium, it called for the Twins to reach a deal with a single host city.

So, even though Governor Jesse Ventura signed the bill, it went nowhere. Over the next two years, the Twins hoped to no avail that the legislature would amend the bill to allow for a partnership.

In May of 2005, the Twins and Hennepin County reached a stadium deal, but much of the general public was upset because there was no referendum on the deal.

In early February of 2006, a Hennepin County district judge ruled that the Twins were not obligated to play in the Metrodome beyond the 2006 season.

After nearly a decade of lobbying for a ballpark, the Twins are finally getting a new home. On the last day of the 2006 session, the Minnesota legislature passed a Twins stadium bill. It passed the house by a vote of 71 to 61 and the senate by a 34-32 vote. The $522-million open-air stadium will be located in downtown Minneapolis near the Target Center. The ballpark will be financed primarily by a sales-tax increase within Hennepin County.

The Twin Cities really dodged a bullet here. If the stadium bill hadn't passed this time, there is no doubt in my mind that the Pohlads would have sold the team. They did not want to be part of moving the Twins to another city, but potential buyers were lined up who would have relocated the team. Commissioner Bud Selig verified that to me after the stadium bill passed. Instead, we will have a beautiful new outdoor ballpark for many years to come.

Gophers Baseball

The man most responsible for putting the University of Minnesota baseball program on the map was Dick Siebert. He coached the Gophers to three NCAA titles (1956, 1960, and 1964) and was one of the greatest college baseball coaches of all time.

After getting started as a player at Concordia Junior College in St. Paul (now Concordia University), Siebert went on to a professional baseball career that spanned twelve seasons in the major leagues, the last eight playing for legendary manager Connie Mack of the Philadelphia Athletics. Siebert left the majors in 1945 and returned to the Twin Cities to become a radio broadcaster for the St. Paul Saints.

At around this same time, I had developed a great relationship with University of Minnesota athletic director Frank McCormick. We used to talk just about every day. One day in 1947, after Dave MacMillan announced he was stepping down as Gopher baseball coach, McCormick said to me, "You know all the answers. Who should I hire as baseball coach?" I told him to hire Dick Siebert. "He won't come here," McCormick replied. I said, "I'll go find out." Siebert took the job.

The Gophers were around .500 for the first few years under Siebert, but in the early 1950s, Paul Giel came along. Siebert always said that Giel was the first player who made him think the Gophers could compete.

The star of the Gophers' 1956 championship team was Jerry Kindall, who went on to play in the major leagues for nine seasons. After retiring from the majors, Kindall had a long and successful career as a college coach. He is the only guy to both play and coach for a team that won the College World Series; he later coached the University of Arizona to a title.

Before becoming the university's athletic director, Frank McCormick coached the Gophers baseball team in the 1930s.

Coach Dick Siebert (far right) led the baseball program to new heights during the 1950s and 1960s.

Dave Winfield

Dave Winfield is one of the greatest all-around athletes ever produced in Minnesota.

After a standout high school career at St. Paul Central High School, Winfield went on to play baseball and basketball at the University of Minnesota. He started out on the baseball team, but after he was spotted playing intramural basketball, he was asked to join coach Bill Musselman's team as well. He was a member of the 1971–72 team that won the Big Ten title and the 1972–73 team, which finished runner-up in the Big Ten.

In baseball, Winfield was named a first-team All-American in 1973 after leading the Gophers to the College World Series. As a pitcher, he set a school record by striking out 109 batters; the record stood until 1997.

In 1973, he was drafted by four teams in three professional sports leagues. The San Diego Padres selected him in the first round, fourth player overall, in Major League Baseball's amateur draft in June. He was also selected by the Vikings in the NFL draft—despite not playing collegiate football—and by teams in both the ABA and the NBA.

After receiving a $15,000 signing bonus from the Padres, Winfield joined the team for the 1973 season. He is one of just a handful of major-league players who never played in the minors. He spent the first eight years of his career with the Padres before signing a big free-agent contract with the New York Yankees. His eight-and-a-half-year tenure with the Yankees was perhaps best known for his tumultuous relationship with owner George Steinbrenner. He was traded to the California Angels early in the 1990 baseball season. In 1992, he signed with the Toronto Blue Jays, where he won a World Series ring. Winfield returned home to Minnesota to play for the Twins in 1993 and 1994. While with the Twins, he collected his 3,000th career hit.

He retired after spending the 1995 season with the Cleveland Indians.

In twenty-two major league seasons, Winfield had 3,110 hits, 465 home runs, and 1,833 RBI. He is just one of five major leaguers in history to have more than 3,000 hits and at least 450 home runs. He also won seven Gold Glove Awards and played in twelve consecutive All-Star Games from 1977 to 1988.

He was elected to the Hall of Fame in 2001—the same year that Kirby Puckett was inducted.

A two-sport star at the university, Dave Winfield was one of the greatest all-around athletes to come out of the state of Minnesota.

The local hero came back to play for his hometown team toward the end of his Hall of Fame career.

Pitcher Paul Giel was one of the first Gophers to have a professional baseball career.

In addition to his three championships, Siebert will go down in history as the only college coach to have recruited and coached two major league players who reached the 3,000-hit mark: David Winfield and Paul Molitor. The Gophers reached the College World Series with Winfield in 1973 and again in 1977 with Molitor. Siebert called Molitor the smartest player he ever coached. The Gophers are one of just a handful of college programs that has two alumni in the Baseball Hall of Fame.

Siebert coached the Gophers until his death in 1978. He posted a career record of 754-360, and at the time he was just one of three college baseball coaches with more than 700 victories.

Siebert's influence on baseball in Minnesota went behind his success as the Gophers coach. He also conducted clinics for kids around the state every summer.

Former Gopher and major leaguer George Thomas took over as the baseball coach in 1979 and coached the Gophers for three seasons. Thomas resigned in the fall of 1981, and assistant coach John Anderson took the reins. At twenty-six years old, he was the youngest coach in Big Ten Conference history.

Anderson has done a great job since taking over as Gophers baseball coach. The team won a Big Ten title in his first season. In twenty-four years, he's never had a losing season; 2005 was the Gophers' forty-third consecutive winning season. In 2003, Anderson passed Siebert to

Paul Molitor

Paul Molitor and Jack Morris are the greatest competitors I've covered.

Molitor, who was an excellent athlete at Cretin High School in St. Paul, was a two-time All-American (in 1976 and 1977) for the University of Minnesota baseball team. Molitor helped the Gophers reach the 1977 College World Series (CWS)—the last time the Gophers have been to the CWS.

In 1977, the Milwaukee Brewers selected Molitor with the third overall pick in the June amateur draft. After one season in the minors, Molitor joined the Brewers and was named the American League Rookie of the Year in 1978.

Molitor played for Milwaukee for fifteen seasons. The Brewers had some great teams during that time. Molitor and Robin Yount helped lead the Brewers to the playoffs for the first time in 1981 and then to the World Series in 1982. In 1987, Molitor put together a thirty-nine-game hitting streak—the ninth-longest in major-league history.

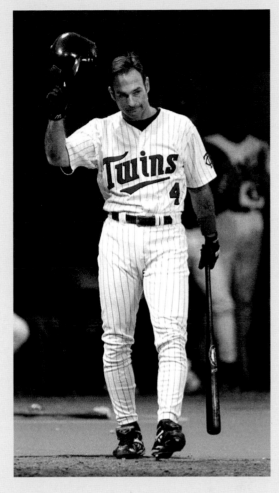

St. Paul native Molitor played for the Twins in his final three seasons in the majors.

Paul Molitor's .375 batting average in 1976 helped him to earn All-American honors at the university. *AP/Wide World Photos*

Molitor went to the Toronto Blue Jays in 1993 and, like Dave Winfield the year before, won a World Series ring. He stayed in Toronto for two more seasons before joining the Twins in 1996. Also like Winfield before him, Molitor got his 3,000th hit while wearing a Twins uniform. He turned forty years old during the 1996 season, but still batted .341 and had 113 runs batted in—becoming the oldest player ever to have more than 100 RBI. He retired following the 1998 season.

In his twenty-one-year career, Molitor had a .306 batting average, 3,319 hits, and more than 500 stolen bases. He missed over 600 games in his career due to injuries. Without the injuries, he might have gotten 4,000 career hits.

In 2004, Paul Molitor was elected to the Hall of Fame in his first year of eligibility.

Coach Dick Siebert congratulates Dave Winfield after a Gophers victory at Bierman Field (now called Siebert Field) in the early 1970s.

Right: John Anderson is the winningest coach in Gophers baseball history.

become the winningest coach in school history. After the 2005 season, he had 871 career victories. His 392 conference wins make him the most successful coach in the history of Big Ten baseball.

As of 2005, thirteen of Anderson's former players have gone on to play in the major leagues: Terry Steinbach, Greg Olson, Tim McIntosh, Bryan Hickerson, Denny Neagle, J. T. Bruett, Dan Wilson, Brent Gates, Brian Raabe, Jeff Schmidt, Kerry Ligtenberg, Jim Brower, and Robb Quinlan.

Left: Another future major leaguer, Jerry Kindall was the shortstop on the Gophers' 1956 championship team.

chapter 3
FOOTBALL

The Greatest Gophers Team

In the 1930s and 1940s, the University of Minnesota football team won five national titles in an eight-year span (1934, 1935, 1936, 1940, and 1941) under coach Bernie Bierman. Gophers football was the biggest story in town during this time. There were six daily newspapers in Minneapolis and St. Paul, and the coverage of Gophers football was unbelievable.

People like to talk about what was the greatest Gophers football team of all time. Despite all the national championship teams, in my opinion the best Gophers team was the 1949 team. A total of twelve Gophers were selected in the 1950 NFL draft, including three in the first round: Clayton Tonnemaker, Leo Nomellini, and Bud Grant. There was also Gordy Soltau, who was taken in the third round, and Floyd Jaszewski, a sixth-round selection. No other Gophers' team had that many top draft picks.

The Gophers started off the 1949 season by winning their first three games, and then headed to Columbus for a road game against Ohio State. Going into the contest, the

Bud Grant brought a lot of intensity in his eighteen years as coach of the Minnesota Vikings.

Gophers were ranked fifth and the Buckeyes were ranked eleventh. The Gophers won easily, 27-0, to improve to 4-0 and move up to number three in the polls.

Coach Bierman was so concerned that the team would be overconfident the next week against Michigan that he worked their butts off in practice during the week leading up to the game.

The Gophers spent the night before the game in a hotel in Jackson, Michigan. On the morning of the game, Bierman was worried that the players were too distracted by the fans and families in the hotel lobby, so he got them to the stadium at 10 a.m. for the game, which was scheduled to begin at 1 p.m.

The Wolverines, who were ranked No. 12, were fired up for the game. There was some "fire Bennie Oosterbaan" talk in Michigan. The Wolverines had won the national championship the previous year in Oosterbaan's first season as coach, but they had lost two straight games—to Army and Northwestern—going into the Gophers game. The Wolverines saved Oosterbaan's job by beating the Gophers, 14-7.

Bud Grant said the Gophers had nervous exhaustion from being in the locker room for three hours before the game. Grant always said that was one lesson he used later when he was a coach: Don't take a team to the locker room too early.

After the Michigan loss, Bierman worked the Gophers even harder the next week to prepare for their home game against Purdue. The Gophers lost that game 13-7.

Coach Bernie Bierman (center) poses proudly with team captain Pug Lund (left) and assistant Sig Harris (right) after winning the Little Brown Jug with a 34-0 victory over Michigan in November 1934.

University President Lou Morrill called Bierman into his office after the Purdue game and told him that he had been getting complaints from parents about how hard he had worked the team.

Bierman told his assistants, "I'll take it easy on the team this week, and that will show them."

The Gophers beat Iowa, 55-7, on the next Saturday after not working at all during the week. They won their last two games to finish the season 7-2.

One thing the Gophers lacked in 1949 was a great running back. They had Billy Bye, who was good, but they nearly had somebody even better. Following the end

Bud Wilkinson was a versatile star for the Gophers' three national championship teams in the 1930s.

of World War II, the Gophers recruited two guys, Bud Grant and Dean Widseth, from the Great Lakes Naval Station team that Paul Brown had coached. Another player from that team, halfback Frank Aschenbrenner, also wanted to play for the Gophers, but the university's faculty representative ruled that he wouldn't immediately be eligible to play at the university because not all of his credits would transfer from his previous school, Marquette. Aschenbrenner ended up at Northwestern, where he helped beat the Gophers twice (in 1946 and 1948) with long runs. Aschenbrenner led Northwestern to the 1949 Rose Bowl and was named MVP of the game after scoring on a seventy-three-yard touchdown run, which helped Northwestern beat California, 20-14. If the

Coach Bierman confers with the Gophers' co-captains, Howie Brennan and Clayton Tonnemaker, at practice during the 1949 season.

Leo Nomellini went on to become a ten-time Pro Bowler in the NFL after his stellar career as a Gopher.

Bud Grant was a four-year letterman on the football team.

Gophers had him, they might have won three consecutive national championships.

Charlie Johnson, the sports editor of the *Star and Tribune*, started ripping Bierman in the paper. Johnson said that Bierman had ruined the 1949 team and should have made the Rose Bowl.

Bierman coached just one more season. In 1950, the Gophers went 1-7-1, after going 7-2 in each of the previous two seasons. Bierman wanted to keep coaching because he wanted to coach Paul Giel, who had played on the freshman team in 1950. But the university administration got some of the former Gopher greats, like Babe LeVoir, to talk Bierman into stepping down.

Bernie Bierman retired as the second-winningest coach in school history. Although the Gophers went just 30-23-1 in his last six seasons as coach, Bierman walked away with a record of 93-35-6 over sixteen seasons.

Rose Bowl Bound: The Warmath Era

ack in the 1940s and 1950s, going to a college football bowl game was a lot more difficult than it is today. There were far fewer games, and usually only the conference champion earned an invitation. Even with the national championships under Bernie Bierman, it wasn't until 1961 and 1962 that the Gophers made an appearance in a bowl game. Then they made back-to-back trips to the "Granddaddy of Them All"—the Rose Bowl.

After Bierman stepped down as coach in 1950, the university's athletic director, Ike Armstrong, went after some big names to fill Bierman's shoes. He approached Paul "Bear" Bryant, who was in his fifth season as coach at the University of Kentucky. In his only public statement about Bryant's visit, Armstrong told the *Minneapolis Tribune*, "Minnesota is interested in Bryant, and Bryant apparently is interested in us." Bryant remained at Kentucky, however,

Wes Fesler took over the coaching job from the legendary Bernie Bierman in 1950.

All-American Paul Giel runs for a touchdown against Pittsburgh in November 1953. He broke his ankle on the play.

and eventually went on to a legendary career at the University of Alabama.

Armstrong also pursued former Gopher player Bud Wilkinson. Wilkinson had just completed his fourth season as coach at the University of Oklahoma, where he had won a conference title in each of his first four seasons and a national championship following the 1950 season.

Wilkinson, whose father lived in the same building as Charlie Johnson, was interested in the job. Yet, in the end, President Lou Morrill didn't want to hire him. Morrill wanted Wes Fesler, the coach and former All-American at Ohio State University, where Morrill had worked before coming to Minnesota.

Armstrong hired Fesler, who lasted only three seasons while compiling a record of 10-13-4. Wilkinson, meanwhile,

remained at Oklahoma and won two more national titles in his seventeen-year career.

Following the 1953 season, Armstrong and the university were looking for a football coach once again.

One guy who wanted the job was Murray Warmath. Warmath was a southern guy—he had just finished his second season at Mississippi State—and it was unusual back then for a guy from the South to get a job at a northern school. Warmath had been an assistant to Army coach Earl Blaik, and Blaik called the University of Minnesota to recommend Warmath.

Warmath was hired for the 1954 season, and by his fourth season in Minnesota, expectations for the Gophers were high. But the 1957 team didn't live up to expectations. It started the season ranked in the top ten and won its first

three games. The Gophers were ranked as high as fourth, but they lost five of their final six games to finish 4-5.

Things got worse in 1958, when the team lost its first seven games and finished 1-8. It really was a tough year because they were in just about every game. Four of their losses were by six points or less. The same thing happened in 1959. They went 2-7, but four of the losses were by eight or fewer points. That was a tough stretch. From mid-season 1957 through the end of the 1959 season, the Gophers won just four of twenty-four games.

Warmath had to endure a lot personally during that time as well. After the 1958 season, he had garbage dumped on his lawn and he was hung in effigy outside one of the dorms on campus. Following that season, Warmath accepted the coaching job at the University of Arkansas. John Barnhill, the school's athletic director, had been a teammate of Warmath's at the University of Tennessee.

Warmath was all set to take the Arkansas job when a local businessman named Don Knutson convinced him to stay. Knutson said he'd help recruit players.

It looked like 1960 was going to be another nightmare year after the Gophers got beaten by their alumni team, 19-7, right before the season started. But the Gophers had talented players, including Sandy Stephens, Bobby Bell,

In his seventh season as coach, Murray Warmath led the Gophers to the national championship in 1960.

These eleven men formed the starting offense for the Gophers' 1960 Rose Bowl squad.

Paul Giel

Paul Giel, Butch Nash, and Dave Winfield are the greatest two-sport athletes that I ever saw at the university.

After playing for the Gophers' freshman football team in 1950, Giel, a Winona native, joined the varsity squad in 1951. Giel went on to become a two-time All-American in both baseball and football.

Giel finished third in the Heisman Trophy voting in 1952—Oklahoma's Billy Vessels won it—and he was runner-up to Notre Dame's Johnny Lattner in the Heisman voting in 1953.

In 1953, Giel probably had his greatest game. He helped the Gophers defeat Michigan, 22-0, and claimed the Little Brown Jug for the first time since 1942. Giel rushed for 112 yards, passed for 169 yards, and intercepted two passes.

On the baseball diamond, Giel was a great pitcher. Gophers baseball coach Dick Siebert always said that Giel was the player who made the program competitive.

During Giel's junior year, Wes Fesler was going to coach in the North South All-Star Game following the Gophers' season. He wanted Giel to play in the game, but according to the NCAA rules at the time, if you played in that all-star game, you were ineligible to participate in any collegiate sports after that. Giel was having some arm troubles that year and Frank Lane, the general manager of the Chicago White Sox, told me that on the basis of his junior year, Giel wasn't going to be offered any money to sign a baseball contract. I talked Giel out of playing in the all-star game and he came back for a great senior year as a pitcher.

Giel ended up signing a baseball contract with the New York Giants for $54,000. Back then, if you signed for more than $50,000, the team had to keep you in the major leagues for two years. This was called the "bonus baby" rule.

The Chicago Bears of the National Football League were also interested in him, as was Winnipeg of the Canadian Football League, but Giel made the right choice with baseball.

Giel's baseball career ended in 1961, after six somewhat limited seasons, and he moved back to the Twin Cities. He went to work for the Vikings as the team's business manager and as an assistant to Max Winter. After two years with the Vikings, he went to work for WCCO radio.

In 1971, one of the University of Minnesota regents called me in and said,

Striking a Heisman-like pose during his senior season, the two-time All-American Paul Giel finished in second place in the Heisman Trophy voting that year.

Giel's success on the pitching mound led him to pursue a career in baseball after leaving the university.

"You know Paul Giel real well. We want to hire Giel as the AD, like Wisconsin did with [former Badgers great] Elroy Hirsch."

Giel was working as WCCO's sports director, and WCCO really wanted to keep him. Giel said it was a tough decision, but he decided to accept the job at the university.

During Giel's tenure, he faced more than his share of challenges and controversies.

In 1975, the Gophers basketball program was put under probation by the NCAA for recruiting violations commited by Coach Bill Musselman. In 1986, under Coach Jim Dutcher, three basketball players were charged with sexual assault in Madison, Wisconsin. (They were later acquitted.)

Then, there was the Luther Darville incident. Darville had been hired by university vice president Frank Wilderson as an administrator in the Office of Minority and Special Student Affairs. In May 1988, Darville was indicted and charged with three felony counts of theft by swindle in the disappearance of $186,000 in university funds. He had allegedly given university funds to student athletes.

Even though Darville said that the university athletic department knew nothing about what he was doing, interim president Richard Sauer didn't like Giel and fired him that July, over the objections of several regents including former governor Wendell Anderson.

Giel really got a bad deal because he had done a great job as athletic director. He took over the job when the department was $500,000 in debt, and he got the financial problems straightened out—basketball and football began making money under Giel. The athletic department was able to build up a reserve of $1.5 million. He also deserves a lot of credit for hiring some good coaches like Lou Holtz, wrestling coach J Robinson, baseball coach John Anderson, basketball coach Jim Dutcher, and hockey coaches Herb Brooks and Doug Woog.

As athletic director, Giel accomplished a lot to improve the university's athletic programs.

On New Year's Day of 1962, Minnesota defeated UCLA in the Rose Bowl. Here Bill Munsey runs for one of the Gophers' three touchdowns in the game.

Tom Brown, and Dick Larson, and the team quickly turned it around.

The Gophers opened the season with a win at Nebraska and went on to win their first seven games. They finished the regular season 8-1. The Gophers were awarded their first national championship since 1941. The Gophers also earned their first trip to a bowl game in school history, but they lost to Washington, 17-7, in the Rose Bowl.

Tom Brown was runner-up in the Heisman Trophy voting—behind Navy's Joe Bellino—but Brown did win the Outland Trophy, which is awarded to the top lineman.

For Warmath, who had several chances to leave Minnesota, the Rose Bowl was a dream come true. He realized that dream again the very next season. The Gophers faced UCLA in the Rose Bowl on January 1, 1962, and won, 21-3.

After the 1962 season, the Gophers were in contention for a third-consecutive Rose Bowl berth. They went into their final regular-season game, at Wisconsin, with a 5-1 record in the Big Ten. The Gophers were ranked No. 5 in the nation and Wisconsin was ranked No. 3. The Badgers won the game, 14-9, to earn the trip to the Rose Bowl.

Warmath coached other strong Gopher teams in the 1960s that were good enough to go to a bowl game, but they didn't get the chance because there were so few bowl games then. They came closest in 1967, when the team finished 6-1—losing only to Purdue—and tied Indiana for the Big Ten title. But Indiana went to the Rose Bowl on a tiebreaker, because the Gophers had been there more recently.

Warmath's career at the University of Minnesota came to an end in 1971, following three consecutive losing seasons from 1969 to 1971. After eighteen seasons, the third-longest coaching tenure in Gophers football history, Warmath left with a record of 87-78-7.

A jubilant Gophers team whoops it up after defeating UCLA in the 1962 Rose Bowl.

Glen Mason Brings Stability to the Program

In forty seasons from 1932 to 1971, the Gophers football team was coached by only four men, and all but six of those years were under Bernie Bierman or Murray Warmath. (George Hauser filled in for Bierman during the war years of 1942–44, and Wes Fesler held the reins for the three seasons between Bierman and Warmath.) In the thirty-five seasons since Warmath retired, six different people held the Gophers coaching job, and only Glen Mason has lasted beyond seven years. Mason is also the only coach since Warmath with a winning percentage above .500, and he led the Gophers to six bowl appearances in his first nine seasons as coach.

In 1971, Paul Giel replaced Marsh Ryman as athletic director and hired Cal Stoll to be the new football coach after Warmath. Stoll was an "M" man who had played for Bernie Bierman in the late 1940s, and as coach he came in and beat some good teams—like Michigan and UCLA. If you throw out three losses to Nebraska, his record was pretty good. In seven seasons, he had two teams win seven games and two other teams that won six games.

In 1977, Stoll's sixth season at the U, the Gophers pulled off one of the biggest victories in school history by defeating top-ranked Michigan, 16-0, in Minneapolis. The Gophers had lost all nine previous meetings with the Wolverines, and they hadn't defeated a ranked team since 1961. Between 1962 and 1977, the Gophers were 0-24-1 against ranked teams. Michigan, which had defeated the Gophers 45-0 the previous year en route to the Big Ten championship and a berth in the Rose Bowl, was 6-0 going into the game against the Gophers and had outscored its opponents, 193-42. The Wolverines hadn't been shut out in ten years.

The victory over the Wolverines improved the Gophers' record to 5-2. Minnesota lost its next two games—to Indiana and Michigan State—but won the final two regular-season games to finish with a 7-4 record. The seven victories earned the Gophers their first bowl berth since 1962. On December 22, the Gophers played the University of Maryland in the Hall of Fame Bowl in Birmingham, Alabama. Maryland defeated Minnesota, 17-7.

Stoll had some pretty exciting players, such as Rick Upchurch and Tony Dungy. He also had a running back named Larry Powell. He might have been the fastest running back in school history, but Powell got sick with French polio and his football career was over after one season.

Cal Stoll led the Gophers to a 39-39 record in seven seasons as coach.

In 1978, the Gophers were 5-5 going into the final game of the season against Wisconsin in Madison. Giel told Stoll, whose career record at that point was 39-38, that if he didn't beat the Badgers he was going to be fired. The Badgers won the game, 48-10, and Stoll was fired.

Joe Salem, who had been a quarterback for the Gophers from 1958 to 1960 and was on the 1961 Rose Bowl team, was hired to replace Stoll. Salem was coaching at Northern Arizona, and he probably made a mistake in taking the Gophers job. He could have had the Army or Kansas jobs. He lasted just five seasons at Minnesota, compiling a 19-35-1 record. The Gophers lost seventeen of their last eighteen Big Ten games under Salem.

After Joe Salem was fired, Vikings assistant coach Les Steckel was one of the candidates for the job. Steckel called me and asked me what I thought about the Gophers job. I told him he'd never win at Minnesota. They had Warmath, Stoll, and Salem, and none of them had been able to win consistently. If I hadn't talked him out of it, he would have quit the Vikings and replaced Salem.

Vikings assistant coach Jerry Burns, who had given Lou Holtz his first coaching job when he hired him as a grad assistant at Iowa, had been telling me for a long time that Holtz wanted to come to Minnesota. I got to know Holtz well through Burns.

Holtz was the coach at Arkansas. In seven seasons at Arkansas, he coached the Razorbacks to six bowl games but didn't get along with athletic director Frank Broyles. He quit and said he wasn't going to coach anymore.

Holtz ended up taking the Minnesota job and inherited a team that had won just one game in the previous year. Nevertheless, he told me, "There's better players here than I had at Arkansas."

One day, Paul Giel went to Holtz and said, "I have a problem with my heart and I'd like you to become the athletic director and football coach." Giel would still be there, but Holtz would run the show.

Lou was really excited about the job, but Nancy Giel changed Paul's mind. She didn't want her husband to give up the job.

Behind the scenes, Jaye Dyer and other boosters tried to get the university to go through with naming Holtz as athletic director. In my book, if Holtz had gotten the A.D. job, he would have stayed here and not gone to Notre Dame.

Wide receiver Rich Upchurch was one of the standouts on Cal Stoll's Gophers.

Then the football program wouldn't have gone through what it did in the late 1980s and most of the 1990s.

Holtz always told me that leaving Minnesota was the "biggest mistake" he ever made.

He was only here for two years, but there were some memorable games including a game against the University

Tony Dungy was the Gophers' starting quarterback from 1973 to 1976. He later returned to Minnesota as the Vikings' defensive coordinator.

Joe Salem had a tough time motivating his Gophers to success in five seasons as head coach.

Lou Holtz worked his players hard in two years as Minnesota coach before moving on to Notre Dame.

of Oklahoma in 1985. The Sooners were ranked No. 3 and had Troy Aikman as quarterback. Oklahoma won the game, 13-7, but two weeks later Oklahoma coach Barry Switzer called Holtz and said, "I don't want to play you again." He wanted out of the game that was scheduled for the next season. They ended up playing in Oklahoma in 1986, and the Sooners routed the Gophers, coached by John Gutekunst, 63-0.

In December of 1985, after the Gophers had gone 6-5 in the regular season and were going to play in a bowl game for

the first time since 1977, Holtz resigned to take the job at Notre Dame.

While he was at the university, Holtz went out and raised more money than any football coach Minnesota has ever had. It got to a point where he embarrassed the University Foundation so much that they sent him a list of places he couldn't go.

A group of businessmen and boosters tried to bring Holtz back to Minnesota as athletic director after Giel was fired in 1988. Notre Dame was getting ready to play West Virginia

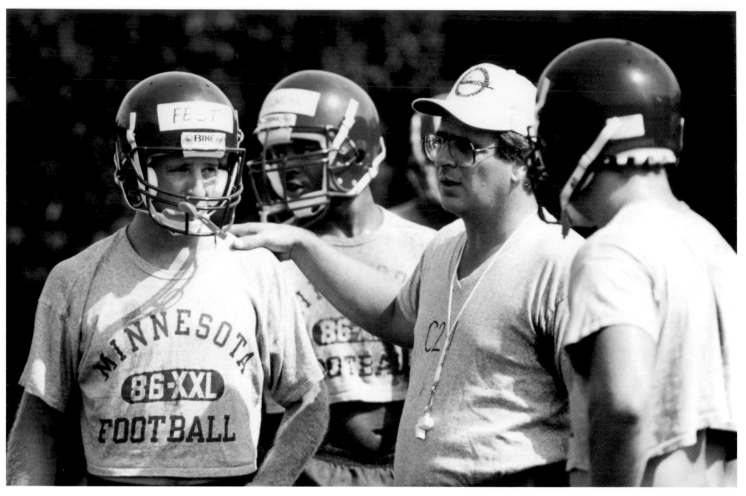

Next in line on Minnesota's coaching carousel was John Gutekunst, who took over on a permanent basis before the 1986 season.

in the Fiesta Bowl. The group urged the new university president, Nils Hasselmo, to wait until after the Fiesta Bowl before hiring anyone so that they could contact Holtz.

The school went ahead and hired Rick Bay, who had earned a great reputation as an administrator at Ohio State and Oregon. Bay was only in Minnesota for a short time, but he was one of the greatest athletic directors the school has had. He had guts. He'd challenge the president. He was tough, and no one could push him around.

Holtz almost became the Vikings coach when he was out of coaching after retiring from Notre Dame in 1996. The board of directors came within one vote of hiring him

Rick Bay was a great athletic director for the university before being hired away by the Cleveland Indians.

Tyrone Carter delivers a hard hit to Oregon's Joey Harrington during the 1999 Sun Bowl. That year, Carter earned the Jim Thorpe Award as the best defensive back in college football.

Center Greg Eslinger, shown here blocking for running back Laurence Maroney, received the Outland Trophy as the top lineman in 2005.

didn't like Gutekunst, and he fired him after the Gophers went 2-9 in 1991.

Jim Wacker was brought in to replace Gutekunst. Wacker had been successful in rebuilding the Texas Christian program and also had success at North Dakota State.

Under Wacker's coaching, the Gophers were unbelievable offensively, but they couldn't stop anybody. They had several big wins in Wacker's five seasons—Iowa to end his first season in 1992, Rose Bowl–bound Wisconsin in 1993, and number twenty-three Syracuse in 1996— but they were just 2-11 against ranked teams during his tenure. In one stretch, the Gophers lost fourteen out of fifteen Big Ten games, and Wacker was fired following the 1996 season. In his best season, the Gophers went 4-7.

Kansas coach Glen Mason had been a candidate for the Gophers coaching job before Wacker was hired in 1992. He flew to Chicago for an interview and told the search committee, "I'm not looking for a job. You guys asked me to come here. You tell me why I should take the job." They couldn't tell him, so he turned it down.

When the university needed a coach to succeed Wacker, athletic director Mark Dienhart went after a lot of people, including Mason. This time, Mason took the job and signed a seven-year contract.

In the six seasons prior to Mason's arrival, the Gophers were just 9-39 in the Big Ten. They weren't very competitive in those thirty-nine losses and were outscored by an average of nineteen points. Under Mason, the Gophers have been more competitive. They've defeated Big Ten powerhouse Ohio State once and Penn State a couple of times. In 2005, they beat Michigan for the first time since 1986.

Mason coached the 2005 season with one year remaining on his contract. Negotiations for a contract extension were tough and went down to the wire. I'm not convinced that University president Robert Bruininks and athletic director Joel Maturi wanted Mason back. In the end, the two sides agreed on a contract extension that will keep Mason as coach through the 2010 season.

The Gophers have been to six bowl games in the past seven seasons. Prior to Mason taking over as coach, the

and he would have taken the job. In 1999, he got back into coaching at South Carolina.

When Holtz left as Gophers coach after the final game of the 1985 regular season, assistant coach John Gutekunst coached the team in the bowl game and led them to a 20-13 comeback victory over the Clemson Tigers in the Independence Bowl. After a brief search, Gutekunst was eventually hired as the permanent coach.

Actually, Gutekunst did a good job. In his first season, 1986, the Gophers went to another bowl game. It was the first time since 1961–62 that they had gone to bowl games in consecutive years.

The team finished with 6-5 records in three of the next four years, including a 5-3 record in the Big Ten in 1990, but they didn't go to a bowl game.

Dan Meinert had taken over for Rick Bay as athletic director on an interim basis after Bay left to become team president of the Cleveland Indians in 1991. Had Bay stayed, Gutekunst might still be coaching this team. But Meinert

Laurence Maroney was the team's leading rusher in 2005, including a 127-yard performance against Ohio State. Maroney and Marion Barber III formed a formidable rushing duo in 2003 and 2004.

Marion Barber III stiff-arms an Alabama defender during Minnesota's 20-16 win in the 2004 Music City Bowl. The Plymouth native ran for 187 yards and scored a touchdown in the game.

Gophers had only been to five bowls in school history. Of course, there are more bowl games being played today, but it's the same opportunity for all of the teams. Indiana, Northwestern, and teams like that haven't been to a lot of bowl games.

Mason has done a good job as the Gophers coach. He's brought stability and respectability to the program. The 2005 season was his ninth as the football coach, the fourth longest tenure in school history, and the longest since Murray Warmath retired in 1971. Only Warmath, Dr. Henry Williams (twenty-two seasons), and Bernie Bierman (sixteen

seasons) have coached the Gophers longer. In the time that Joe Paterno has been Penn State's head coach (the 2005 season was his fortieth season as the coach of the Nittany Lions), the Gophers have had seven coaches.

Mason has made the team competitive despite the fact that the Gophers have one of the lowest football budgets in the Big Ten. A lot of people think the reason Wisconsin and Iowa win is that they have better coaching. I don't think coaching has anything to do it. I think in Iowa City, that's all they've got. In the whole state of Iowa, it's the Hawkeyes, Iowa State, and a few Division I schools. They have no pros there. Here, the Gophers have to compete with the Vikings as well as professional baseball, basketball, and hockey teams.

Luring the Vikings:
Pro Football Comes to the Twin Cities

Just as Minnesota struggled to lure Major League Baseball during the pre-expansion era, professional football was another elusive goal for the state. The NFL consisted of just ten teams in the late 1940s, including two teams in Chicago and two in New York.

I used to bug John Mara, owner of the New York Giants, about getting an NFL team in the Twin Cities. I first met him when the Giants held training camp in Superior, Wisconsin, in the late 1930s. Minneapolis had two pro football teams that had failed in the early days of the NFL (the Minneapolis Marines from 1921 to 1924, and the Minneapolis Red Jackets in 1929 and 1930), and Mara would always say that the Gophers were just too big and we'd never have a pro team.

During the 1950s, an annual NFL exhibition game sponsored by Catholic Charities was held in the Twin Cities. The Pittsburgh Steelers played in the game in 1956 and had been guaranteed $15,000. It rained the day of the game, which hurt attendance. When the priest presented Steelers owner Art Rooney with the check for the Steelers' guarantee, he asked Rooney to hold the check for a month before cashing it. Rooney tore the check up.

For the most part, the exhibitions were successful and gave business leaders in the Twin Cities further impulse to try to get a professional football team.

In 1959, the Star and Tribune Company decided to bring two regular-season games to the Twin Cities to show

Bert Rose (right) was named as general manager of the new Minnesota football team by owner Bill Boyer in August 1960.

Ole Haugsrud sat on the Vikings' board of directors for sixteen years and was its first chairman.

Chicago Bears owner George Halas was instrumental in getting an NFL team in Minnesota.

that the area could support an NFL team. Gerry Moore of the Minneapolis Chamber of Commerce and I went to Chicago and guaranteed the Chicago Cardinals $125,000 to play at Met Stadium. The Cardinals were thinking about moving from Chicago, and we thought we could get them to move here. (The Cardinals moved to St. Louis after the 1959 season.)

Metropolitan Stadium was packed for both of the Cardinals games that fall, and the games made money.

At the time, professional football was going through the same situation as baseball—where major league owners had dragged their feet about expanding, and as a result, a third major league was threatening to form.

The NFL hadn't expanded since 1950, when it accepted three teams from the short-lived All-American Football Conference: the Cleveland Browns, Baltimore Colts, and San Francisco 49ers. In August 1959, a new professional football league called the American Football League (AFL),

was formed. It was going to start play in 1960 with eight teams, including clubs in New York, Los Angeles, Houston, Dallas, Denver, Buffalo, and Boston.

Max Winter, who had left the Minneapolis Lakers because he thought being involved with basketball would kill his aspirations of owning a football team, announced that he, William Boyer, and H. P. Skoglund were going to pursue an AFL team for Minneapolis and St. Paul.

The AFL scheduled its first official league meeting for late November 1959 in Minneapolis. The league's first draft of college players was scheduled to start on Monday, November 23, and Winter was the chairman of the league's draft committee.

As the owners gathered in town on Sunday the 22nd—the same day that the NFL's Chicago Cardinals and New York Giants played before 26,625 fans at Metropolitan Stadium—a rumor was going around that the Minneapolis–St. Paul group would withdraw from the AFL because it was going to be granted an NFL expansion team.

Norm Van Brocklin (left) signed on as the Vikings' first coach early in 1961.

That Sunday night, the AFL owners had an emergency meeting at the Nicollet Hotel that lasted well into Monday morning. While the meeting was going on, an early edition of Monday's *Minneapolis Tribune* was brought into the meeting. It featured a story that said the Twin Cities were going to get an NFL team.

Charlie Johnson's story said that ten of the twelve NFL owners had agreed to award the Twin Cities an expansion franchise to begin in 1960.

This change threw the whole meeting into turmoil. Max Winter walked out before the meeting ended and said that he was withdrawing from the group because public sentiment favored the Twin Cities getting an NFL team.

Boyer and Skoglund decided to go ahead with bringing an AFL franchise here, and when the league's draft started on Monday, Boyer and Skoglund drafted players for the Minneapolis franchise. After meeting for several days, the league announced that the meeting would continue in Dallas in early December.

On November 30, the owners announced that former South Dakota governor and World War II hero Joe Foss would be the American Football League's first commissioner. The league had first approached University of Michigan athletic director Fritz Crisler, who had coached the Gophers football team for two years during the 1930s, but Crisler was not interested in the job.

At the meeting in Dallas, Foss recommended to the owners that they allow the Minneapolis–St. Paul group to leave. To replace the Minnesota franchise, Oakland was awarded a franchise.

Meanwhile, the NFL owners were scheduled to meet in Miami in January of 1960 to deal with the matter of expansion and to find a replacement for Commissioner Bert Bell, who had passed away the previous October.

When the owners convened, they named Pete Rozelle, then general manager of the Los Angeles Rams, as the league's new commissioner. The expansion issue faced a major obstacle. The NFL's constitution had to be amended to say that the league could expand if ten of the twelve team owners voted yes, instead of requiring a unanimous vote. One owner— the Washington Redskins' George Preston Marshall—was opposed to expansion and he threatened to sue.

Chicago Bears owner George Halas, who was the head of the expansion committee, was able to convince the other owners to amend the constitution, and on January 28, the National Football League announced that it was expanding with two new teams. Dallas would join the league in 1960 and Minnesota would follow in 1961.

In June 1960, the AFL filed a $10 million lawsuit against the NFL in federal district court in Washington, D.C. Among the charges in the lawsuit, which called the NFL a monopoly, was that the NFL granted new franchises in territories where the AFL already had made commitments.

Halas was called to testify at the trial. He was asked about stealing the Minnesota franchise from the AFL. Halas said if someone was driving you as crazy as I drove him, you'd give him a franchise to just get him off your back. I had been the contact guy with Halas for Skoglund, Winter, and Boyer. When they first started pursuing a football team, Halas kept telling us to be patient, but for a long time it didn't look like the NFL would ever expand. So, when the AFL came along, they listened. But it came down to taking a gamble on a start-up league like the AFL, which nobody thought would last more than a couple of years, or try to get in the NFL.

The Minnesota NFL team named its board of directors in early August 1960. Boyer was named president and Winter was named vice president. Skoglund and Bernie Ridder Jr. were the other officers.

Coach Van Brocklin, general manager Bert Rose, and the Vikings players celebrated victory following the franchise's inaugural game on September 17, 1961.

Ole Haugsrud was named chairman of the board. Haugsrud had owned the Duluth Eskimos of the NFL in the 1920s and then sold the team at a league meeting in 1930 for $3,000. He was promised that he would get the first bid for the next NFL franchise in Minnesota.

The first move the group made was to hire Bert Rose as the team's general manager. Rose had been the public relations director for the Los Angeles Rams. Both Dan Reeves, who owned the Rams, and the new league commissioner Pete Rozelle, who also worked with Rose in Los Angeles, praised the selection.

In November, the team announced that it was going to be called the Minnesota Vikings. Winter had always liked that name. In 1947, he had wanted to call the Minneapolis basketball team the Vikings, but instead they decided to call it the Lakers, of course.

Rose started interviewing candidates for the coaching position in December 1960. The first person he interviewed was Northwestern coach Ara Parseghian, but Rose never offered him the job. Rose clearly wanted to hire Norm Van Brocklin from the start. Van Brocklin had played for the Rams while Rose was with the team.

Winter had wanted to hire Bud Grant, who was coaching Winnipeg of the Canadian Football League (CFL). Grant initially turned Winter and Rose down, but Winter thought he could still convince Grant to take the job.

Rose was able to get several members of the board to agree with him, and they hired the thirty-four-year-old Van Brocklin as the team's first coach. At the time, Winter was very bitter about the decision.

Van Brocklin had just retired as a player following the 1960 season after winning the league's Most Valuable Player Award and leading the Philadelphia Eagles to the NFL championship. It was the third championship team that Van Brocklin had played for in his career.

The Vikings took part in their first player draft on December 27, 1960. With their first pick, they took Tulane halfback Tommy Mason. In the second round, they took North Carolina linebacker Rip Hawkins. Their third-round selection was Georgia quarterback Fran Tarkenton. In the fifth round, they picked defensive back Ed Sharockman. It was a pretty good first draft for the Minnesota Vikings franchise.

The Vikings played their first regular-season game on September 17, 1961, at Metropolitan Stadium. The Vikings upset George Halas and the Chicago Bears, 37-13. Tarkenton came off the bench to pass for 250 yards and four touchdowns.

At first, Winter didn't have much to do as the team vice president. Then Boyer started having some personal problems and Winter took over. After that, Rose resigned as general manager in June 1964. The team hired Jim Finks, who had been president of the Calgary team in the CFL, to replace Rose.

Throughout the early years, coach Van Brocklin and quarterback Tarkenton did not get along. Van Brocklin attempted to quit more than once, but Bernie Ridder talked him out of it each time. In 1966, as the feuding continued, Tarkenton asked to be traded.

After the 1966 season, Van Brocklin quit again, and this time Ridder decided to let him go. Van Brocklin resigned in February 1967; in 1968, he became the coach of the Atlanta Falcons.

The team went ahead and traded Tarkenton, too. On March 7, 1967, one month after Van Brocklin resigned, Tarkenton was traded to the New York Giants for four draft choices. That trade turned out to be great for the Vikings.

Max Winter served on the Vikings' board from its founding until his retirement in 1989. He was also the team's president from 1965 to 1987.

The team used those draft picks to take running back Clinton Jones, receiver Bob Grim, and offensive linemen Ron Yary and Ed White.

Three days after trading Tarkenton, Winter named a new coach and a new era in Minnesota football had begun.

Super Bowl Dreams: The Bud Grant Era

Within the span of the franchise's first decade, the Minnesota Vikings went from hapless expansion team with a record of 5-22-1 over its first two seasons to championship contenders. They went from having the lowest-ranked defense in the league in 1961 and 1962 to the top-ranked defense for three years running (1969–71). In addition to building a foundation of core players, the team brought in a coach who really turned the team around.

There never was any doubt in the minds of Max Winter and general manager Jim Finks who they would hire after Van Brocklin resigned. When Bud Grant walked into the old Holiday Inn Airport in Bloomington to be introduced as the successor to Van Brocklin, it was one of Winter's proudest moments with the Vikings.

When the offer was first made, Grant almost said no again to Winter. Grant had just signed a new three-year deal to be the coach and general manager of the Winnipeg CFL team. But he accepted the Vikings' offer because of Finks and Winter. Grant had been close to Winter since their days with the Minneapolis Lakers, and he knew Finks from the Canadian Football League.

I think the turning point for the Vikings organization came in the second week of the 1968 season—the franchise's eighth season and Grant's second as coach. The team went into Milwaukee and defeated the defending-champion Green Bay Packers, 26-13. The team seemed to get going from that point, and they made the playoffs for the first time.

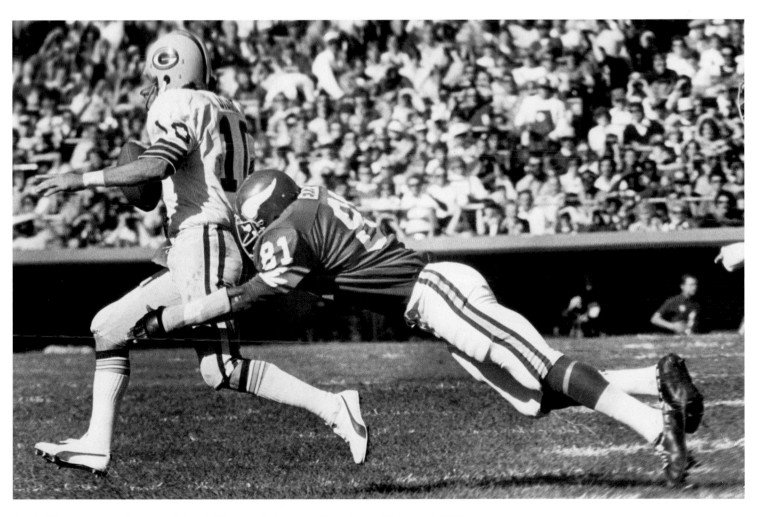

Carl Eller was the heart of the Vikings' defensive line from 1964 to 1978.

Alan Page and the rest of the Purple People Eaters struck fear in the hearts of opposing quarterbacks.

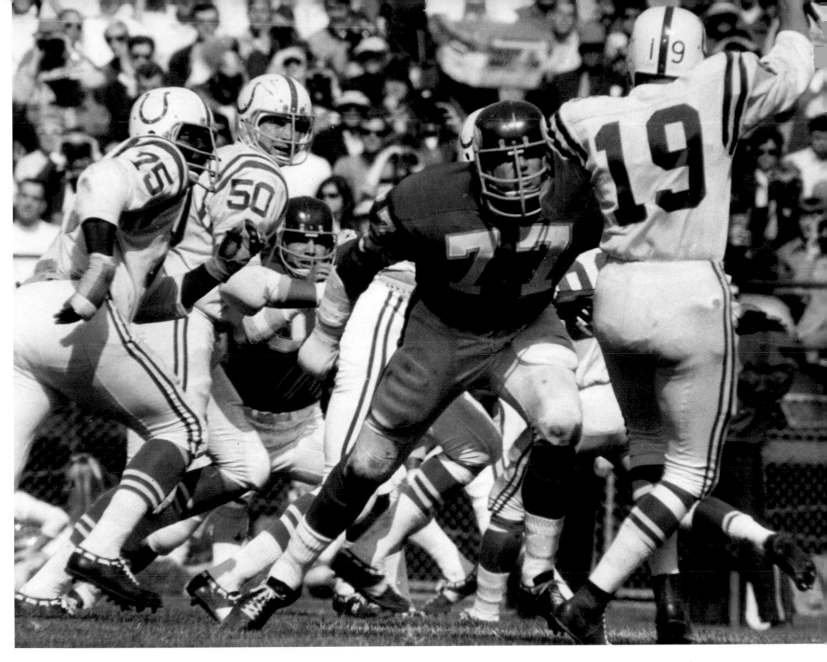

One of Minnesota's four Pro Bowl–bound defensive linemen in 1969, Gary Larsen stares down Baltimore Colts quarterback Johnny Unitas.

The Vikings dominated the league in the mid-1970s. The team's defensive line of Jim Marshall, Carl Eller, Alan Page, and Gary Larsen—the Purple People Eaters—proved that defense is the most important thing in football. Page, when he was at the proper weight, was one of the greatest football players of all time. A nine-time Pro Bowler, he was named the league MVP by the Associated Press in 1971.

The legendary San Francisco 49ers coach Bill Walsh is always given credit for coming up with the so-called West Coast Offense. One night when I was driving home from a speech, I was listening to the radio and Walsh was being interviewed on some nighttime sports show. Somebody asked him where he got the West Coast Offense, and Walsh said, "I stole it from Jerry Burns. The Vikings found out that a five-yard pass from Tarkenton to Chuck Foreman was as good as a five-yard run."

That's the West Coast Offense: the short passing game. Jerry Burns was the Vikings' offensive coordinator from 1968 to 1985, before taking over as head coach in 1986. There was no greater offensive coordinator than Jerry Burns. He was the smartest offensive football guy who ever lived. When he was an assistant coach at Iowa, he took the Wing-T Offense and

On December 9, 1979, Jim Marshall played his final game at Met Stadium, after nineteen seasons as a Viking.

In 1969, Grant's third season as head coach, the Vikings went 12-2. Their losses, both on the road, came in the first week of the season against the Giants and in the final week of the season against the Atlanta Falcons. In between, they won twelve consecutive games, including two shutouts, and never gave up more than two touchdowns in a game.

The Vikings defeated the Los Angeles Rams and then the Cleveland Browns in the first two rounds of the 1969 playoffs. They met the Kansas City Chiefs in a Super Bowl matchup on January 11, 1970. Although the Chiefs were considered underdogs going into the game, they had a great team. Owner Lamar Hunt spent a lot of money to sign all of those superstars—including former Gopher Bobby Bell and fellow future Hall of Famers Buck Buchanan, Len Dawson, Willie Lanier, and Jan Stenerud—and he hired coach Hank Stram, another Hall of Famer. The Vikings lost to the Chiefs, 23-7.

After that first trip to the Super Bowl, the Vikings suffered first-round playoff losses in each of the next two seasons. In those seasons, the Vikings used three different starting quarterbacks: Gary Cuozzo, Bobby Lee, and Norm Snead. In January 1972, the Vikings re-acquired Fran Tarkenton from the New York Giants. They traded Snead, wide receiver Bob Grim, running back Vince Clements, and two future first-round draft choices to get Tarkenton back. In his first season back with the team, the Vikings were just 7-7 and missed the playoffs. In 1973, they rebounded with a 12-2 record and the first of three Super Bowl appearances in four seasons with Tarkenton as quarterback. In 1975, Tarkenton was named the league's MVP after passing for nearly 3,000 yards and twenty-five touchdowns.

Super Bowl IV marked the first of four Super Bowl losses for the Vikings in less than a decade. The teams that the Vikings played in those games were probably four of the greatest teams ever to play in the Super Bowl.

In Super Bowl VIII, the Vikings lost to the Miami Dolphins. The Dolphins, who were run by Minneapolis lawyer Joe Robbie, were playing in their third consecutive Super Bowl and coming off an undefeated season in 1972. Miami was coached by Don Shula, and six members of the team went on to the Hall of Fame: quarterback Bob Griese, fullback Larry Csonka, linebacker Nick Buoniconti, center Jim Langer (a Minnesota native), guard Larry Little, and wide receiver Paul Warfield.

Then, in Super Bowl IX, the Vikings lost to the Pittsburgh Steelers. The Steelers were a legendary team that won four Super Bowls in a six-year span. The Steelers team that beat the Vikings had nine players—Terry Bradshaw, Franco

made it better. He was a consultant to Bud Grant in Winnipeg and installed the Wing-T there. When he was an assistant with the Vikings, coaches from all over the country visited the Vikings' complex to learn about the offense. He had more friends in the coaching business than anybody I've known.

On the offensive side of the field, Chuck Foreman was the Vikings' top rusher from 1973 to 1978.

Oscar Reed was Minnesota's rushing leader in Super Bowl VIII, but he managed only thirty-two yards against Miami's stingy defense.

Harris, John Stallworth, Lynn Swann, Mike Webster, Mel Blount, Joe Greene, Jack Ham, and Jack Lambert, plus coach Chuck Noll—who are now in the Hall of Fame.

In Super Bowl XI, the Vikings lost to the Oakland Raiders by a final score of 32-14. Coached by John Madden, five members of that Raiders team were later inducted into the football Hall of Fame: Fred Biletnikoff, Willie Brown, Ted Hendricks, Art Shell, and Gene Upshaw. It was Minnesota's third Super Bowl in four years. In the Oakland and Miami games, the Vikings had an opportunity to score early and turn those games around, but in both instances they fumbled on the one- or two-yard line.

Between 1974 and 1977, the Vikings probably had their best team during the one year when they failed to make the Super Bowl. After two consecutive Super Bowl appearances, Minnesota started the 1975 season with ten straight victories. The Vikings finished with a 12-2 record and gave up just 180 points on the season. They were expected to go to the Super Bowl again.

In the first round of the playoffs, the Vikings hosted the Dallas Cowboys at Metropolitan Stadium. The Cowboys won, 17-14, with the help of two controversial calls by the officials. On the first, Dallas was marching down the field, and on one pass completion, it appeared that the Cowboys receiver was out of bounds; the films showed the receiver was indeed out of bounds by about two feet, but the officials missed it. The second controversial play came on the "Hail Mary" pass from Roger Staubach to Drew Pearson.

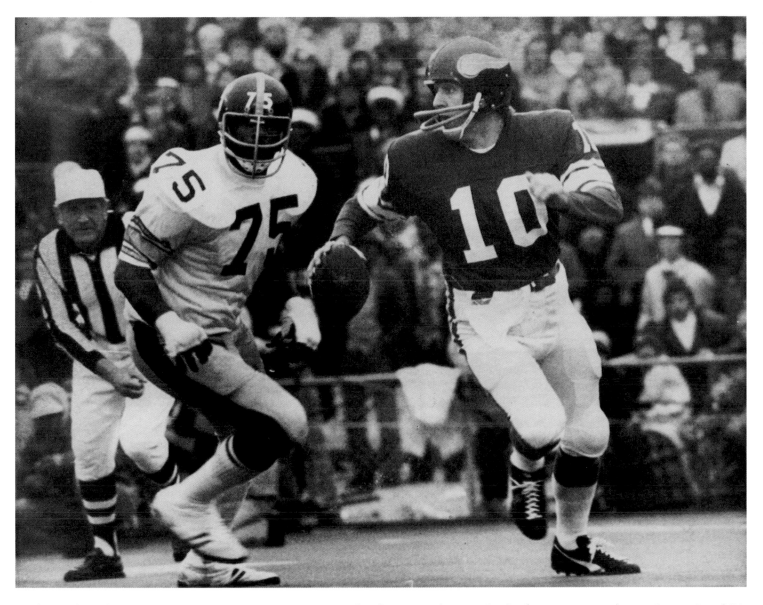

With Pittsburgh's Mean Joe Greene in pursuit, quarterback Fran Tarkenton looks for a receiver during Super Bowl IX.

Everybody thought Pearson pushed off on the play and should have been called for offensive pass interference, but the officials didn't blow the whistle.

By the end of the 1976 season and the fourth Super Bowl loss, many of the Vikings' key players were getting older and the team's fortunes started going downhill after that. The Vikings reached the NFC championship game again following the 1977 season, but they lost to Dallas, 23-6. It was their last appearance in the NFC title game for ten years. They did reach the playoffs three more times under Bud Grant, but they ceased to be the dominant Purple People Eaters of the early and mid-1970s.

In January of 1984, following an 8-8 season, Grant announced that he was retiring after seventeen years as the team's coach. He did return as coach for the 1985 season (following a disastrous 3-13 season under Les Steckel, who had been one of Grant's assistants), but the team finished 7-9 and missed the playoffs for the third year in a row.

Although he may be remembered by some as the coach who lost four Super Bowls, Bud Grant led the Vikings to a 158-96-5 record as coach. In the eleven-year span from 1968 to 1978, the Vikings won the NFL Central Division title ten times in addition to their four Super Bowl trips. They haven't been back to the Super Bowl since Grant's departure.

Super Bowl City: The Super Bowl Comes to the Metrodome

I'm one guy who never thought the Super Bowl would ever come to Minneapolis.

The 1982 Super Bowl was played at the Pontiac Silverdome in suburban Detroit. The weather was bad and the organization was terrible. The only reason Detroit had been given the game was that the automotive companies were big NFL sponsors and they put on the pressure. The feeling was that there would never be another Super Bowl played in the North.

Mike Lynn pushed through a motion at an NFL meeting in 1985 stating that one of the next five Super Bowls awarded had to be in North—either Seattle, Minneapolis, or Detroit. With a capacity of just over 63,000 and smaller than both Seattle's Kingdome and Detroit's Superdome, the Metrodome would be the smallest stadium ever to host the Super Bowl.

I didn't think the Metrodome had a chance because of its size, but in May 1989, the league awarded Super Bowl XXVI to Minneapolis for January 1992. A lot of people take the credit for bringing the Super Bowl to Minneapolis.

Former *Tribune* sportswriter Dave Mona, who owned a public relations firm, helped prepare the presentation to the Super Bowl committee. One of the smartest things he did was include a video of Max Winter sitting in an empty Metrodome. "You remember me. I'm Max Winter. Yes, Winter like summer," he said on the video. He went on to make a convincing plea to bring the Super Bowl here.

Marilyn Nelson was chairman of the Twin Cities Super Bowl group and really won people over.

The game was played on January 26, 1992, with 63,130 people in attendance. The Washington Redskins defeated the Buffalo Bills, 37-24.

Despite its relatively small size, the Metrodome proved to be a fine site for Super Bowl XXVI.

Blockbuster Deals . . . and Disappointment

The Minnesota Vikings stumbled out of the Bud Grant era looking to build a core group of players to carry them back to championship contention. A blockbuster bust of a trade, some heartbreaking losses, and off-the-field controversy conspired to define the team's fortunes in a different light over the past two decades.

The Vikings should have named assistant coach Jerry Burns as the new head coach right away after Grant retired. Instead, they went with Les Steckel. No doubt about it, Steckel was a good offensive mind. Yet, a lot of guys can be a No. 2 or a No. 3 guy but not a No. 1 guy. Steckel was one of those guys.

I think general manager Mike Lynn encouraged Steckel. Steckel thought that Grant hadn't worked the Vikings hard enough. So, Steckel made up his mind to work them harder. He ran training camp like it was a Marine boot camp.

Steckel's Vikings went 3-13 in 1984—the franchise's worst record since their second year in the league—and Grant came out of retirement to coach the Vikings for one more season in 1985.

When Grant retired the second time, the Vikings named Burns as head coach. Burns had almost left the Vikings to join Marty Schottenheimer's staff in Cleveland when Steckel got the head coaching job two years earlier, but Burns' family didn't want to move and he stayed.

Burns did a great job as the Vikings' head coach under the circumstances. In his second season, the Vikings reached the NFC championship game for the first time in ten years, but they lost to the Washington Redskins, 17-10.

Perhaps the most significant development during Burns' tenure as coach was the notorious trade engineered by general manager Mike Lynn during the 1989 season.

When general manager Jim Finks left the Vikings following the 1973 season to join the Chicago Bears front office, Max Winter decided not to hire a new general manager but to take on the responsibilities himself. Winter didn't know how to negotiate a contract, so he brought in Mike Lynn as an assistant. Lynn and Winter had gotten to know each other at league meetings when Lynn was lobbying to get an expansion team in Memphis.

After one year as assistant general manager, Lynn became the general manager and executive vice president of the Vikings. Lynn did a great job running the team and he kept it profitable. He also stood up for Winter as president when some on the board of directors thought he should retire.

But whatever else he did, Lynn is most remembered for the Herschel Walker trade. Lynn thought that the trade for the star running back would win the Super Bowl for the Vikings. Rumors started early in the 1989 season that the Dallas Cowboys were interested in trading Walker and that the Vikings were interested.

The unenviable task of following the highly successful Coach Grant fell to Les Steckel. He lasted just one season as head coach.

Jerry Burns finally got his shot to be head coach in 1986. He led the Vikings to the NFC finals in his second season.

Head coach Jerry Burns thought they were offering too much for Walker, but Lynn really wanted him. Lynn ended up trading five players and eight draft choices to the Cowboys for Walker. For the next three seasons, the Vikings didn't have any first- or second-round draft picks.

Walker joined the Vikings in Week Six of the 1989 season and he went crazy in his first game with the team. He rushed for 148 yards and returned two kickoffs for 40 yards. Suddenly, everybody thought that Walker was going to lead the Vikings to the Super Bowl.

The Vikings went 7-4 after the trade, and they did go on to win the NFC Central Division—their first division title

Coach Burns (left) and G.M. Mike Lynn (right) were all smiles at the press conference to welcome the newest Viking, Herschel Walker, in October 1989.

The media swarmed around Walker after he helped lead the Vikings to victory over the Green Bay Packers in his first game with the team.

since 1980—but they were defeated by the San Francisco 49ers, 41-13, in the first round of the playoffs. Then the Vikings missed the playoffs in the next two seasons, and Walker was released after the 1991 season.

With three games remaining in 1991, Burns announced that he would retire at the end of the season. In their search for a replacement, the Vikings narrowed the choices to Stanford University coach Denny Green and Pete Carroll, who had been a Vikings assistant coach from 1985 to 1989.

Bud Grant highly recommended Carroll, but the guy who sold team president Roger Headrick on Green was Bill Walsh. Walsh—whom Green had worked for in three seasons as an assistant coach in San Francisco—convinced Headrick to hire Green. The league got involved as well because they really wanted another minority head coach in the NFL.

On January 10, 1992, Dennis Green was named the fifth coach in franchise history, and just the second African American head coach in the NFL's modern era (after Art Shell of the Los Angeles Raiders).

Walker gained over a thousand total yards for Minnesota in 1990, but the team missed the playoffs for the first time since 1986.

Green earned a Gatorade shower following the 27-7 victory over the Packers in the final game of his first season as coach.

The Vikings' fortunes improved after Green became coach. The team had made the playoffs only five times between 1979 and 1991, and it went 8-8 in Burns' final year as coach.

In Green's first season, the Vikings won seven of their first nine games and finished with an 11-5 record. They won the NFC Central Division title to advance to the playoffs.

The Vikings reached the playoffs in eight of Green's first nine seasons as coach.

The 1998 season—the first with Red McCombs as the team's owner—was remarkable. The Vikings went 4-0 in the preseason and then opened the regular season with seven consecutive victories. After the winning streak was broken by the Tampa Bay Buccaneers (27-24 in Tampa on November 1), the Vikings won their final eight games to finish 15-1.

With an offense anchored by quarterback Randall Cunningham, wide receiver Randy Moss, and running back Robert Smith, the Vikings scored an NFL-record 556 points and earned a first-round bye in the playoffs. They beat Arizona, 41-21, to advance to the NFC Championship Game for the first time in eleven years.

Everyone thought this team was headed to the Super Bowl, but they lost at home to the Atlanta Falcons in overtime. The Vikings were eleven-point favorites going into the game. Late in the first half, they looked to be in control and were leading 20-7. Then the Falcons recovered a fumble at the Vikings' fourteen-yard line and scored on the next play to pull within 20-14. The Vikings were up 20-17 after three quarters and then scored early in the fourth quarter to take a 27-17 lead. Leading 27-20 midway through the fourth quarter, the Vikings drove to the Falcons' twenty-one-yard line— using up four minutes on the clock—and lined up for a field goal. Vikings kicker Gary Anderson, who hadn't missed a kick—extra point or field goal—all season long, missed the thirty-eight-yard field goal. The Falcons got the ball back and scored with forty-nine seconds remaining to tie the game. The Vikings had the ball twice in overtime, but Atlanta finally took over at their own nine-yard line with 8:28 remaining. The Falcons drove to the Vikings' twenty-one-yard line and Morten Anderson kicked a game-winning, thirty-eight-yard field goal. The Vikings were short-handed in the extra period—defensive lineman John Randle and linebacker Ed McDaniel both missed the overtime with injuries—but the high-scoring Vikings offense had scored only seven points after halftime.

The Vikings bounced back and made the playoffs as a Wild Card team in 1999, and then they won the division in 2000 with an 11-5 record. They beat the New Orleans Saints in the playoffs to advance to NFC Championship Game once again. In that game, they got trounced by the New York Giants, 41-0.

The next season—Green's tenth as head coach—the Vikings struggled. They were 5-10 with one game remaining when ESPN reported that Green was going to be fired. Green had told me about a week before this that he was going to resign, but I didn't believe him.

In the end, the Vikings took away Green's power. His contract didn't specifically give him the right to be in charge of the entire football operation, including the draft. But after McCombs took over in 1998, he gave Green the authority. Then McCombs wanted to take it away again after the 2001 season. McCombs also wanted Green to reassign longtime assistant Richard Solomon, who was the inside linebackers coach and director of pro personnel. Green didn't want to do that because Solomon was a close friend.

Dennis Green quit as Vikings head coach on January 4, 2002, with one game left to play in the season. He wasn't

With all-star receivers Cris Carter and Randy Moss to pass to, veteran quarterback Randall Cunningham helped lead the Vikings to a 15-1 record in 1998.

The explosive Moss emerged as one of the league's best in 1998, but he eventually wore out his welcome in Minnesota.

fired. He accepted a buyout of the two years remaining on his contract. He could have stayed, but he wanted to run the team his way. He didn't think he could win under McCombs.

In the ten seasons under Green, the Vikings won four division titles and reached the playoffs eight times. They were 97-62 under Green, and 36-12 between 1998 and 2000.

Mike Tice coached the Vikings in the final game of the 2001 season, a 19-3 loss to Baltimore on Monday Night Football. Several days later, Tice was named as the new head coach. He was signed to a four-year contract, and the team reached the playoffs in only one of those four seasons under Tice.

In March of 2005, the Vikings traded Randy Moss to Oakland in exchange for linebacker Napoleon Harris and two draft picks. In seven seasons with Minnesota Vikings, Moss caught 574 passes for 9,142 yards and 90 touchdowns. He had more receiving yards in his first seven seasons than any other player in NFL history. The controversies and other issues surrounding Moss, however, got a lot of attention in the media, and I think the Vikings were also

Although he never received much national acclaim, Robert Smith was a premier running back for eight seasons before walking away from the game at the age of twenty-eight in 2001.

Playing at home against the San Diego Chargers, receiver Cris Carter pulls in one of his league-high thirteen touchdowns in 1999.

concerned about his health. Moss had chronic ankle problems that went back to his college days. Owner Red McCombs had concluded that, in order for the team to be successful, they couldn't keep both Moss and Tice. He said that he almost fired Tice and kept Moss, but he ultimately decided that by trading Moss, whom he considered one of the top players in the league, he was showing confidence in Coach Tice. Tice might deny it, but I think he wanted to trade Moss too. If they hadn't traded Moss, they wouldn't have had the money to sign free agents Darren Sharper, Fred Smoot, and Pat Williams.

The 2005 season was a turbulent one for the Vikings. Early in the year, Tice, who was going into the final year of

his contract, was fined $100,000—the largest fine ever levied against an NFL coach—for scalping his Super Bowl tickets, which was a violation of league policy.

On the field, the Vikings struggled at the start and won just two of their first six games. The season appeared hopeless when they lost to the Carolina Panthers, 38-13, in their seventh game, and quarterback Daunte Culpepper suffered a season-ending knee injury.

The Vikings did manage to pull off six consecutive wins after the Carolina game and improved to 8-5 with three games left in the season. Back-to-back losses to Pittsburgh and Baltimore, however, eliminated them from playoff contention.

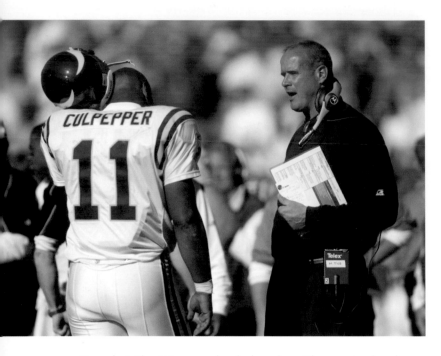

Coach Mike Tice worked closely with quarterback Daunte Culpepper for four years. Both were gone after the 2005 season.

They beat the division-champion Chicago Bears, 34-10, in the final regular-season game.

About an hour after the game, Tice was fired as coach. His record in four seasons was 32-33. The Vikings had a lot of injuries in 2005, and I thought Tice deserved the chance to return as coach.

Owner Zygi Wilf acted quickly to find a replacement. Five days after firing Tice, the Vikings named Philadelphia Eagles assistant coach Brad Childress as the Vikings' seventh head coach. Childress was one of the four people who were interviewed for the job. The other three were Kansas City Chiefs offensive coordinator Al Saunders; Vikings defensive coordinator Ted Cottrell; and Indianapolis Colts quarterback coach Jim Caldwell. It was obvious that once they interviewed Childress, he was their man. Childress had coached in four consecutive NFC championship games with Philadelphia. Prior to joining the Eagles, Childress had been an assistant coach at the University of Wisconsin for eight seasons. Childress and coach Barry Alvarez helped turn the Wisconsin program around. When Childress and Andy Reid took over the Eagles, they were having a lot of trouble beating anybody.

With his ability to both pass and run, Daunte Culpepper was a three-time Pro Bowler with Minnesota.

Vikings Ownership Disputes

While the Vikings' on-the-field fortunes followed a bit of a roller-coaster path in the 1980s and 1990s, the situation in the owners' office was no more stable. After more than twenty-five years as the owner and president, Max Winter sold his interest in the team to Carl Pohlad and Irwin Jacobs in 1987. Although the buyout of Winter's shares gave Pohlad and Jacobs fifty-one percent of the team's stock, they did not have a majority of the voting stock. They didn't agree with the moves that general manager Mike Lynn was making, which led to several years of ownership disputes.

In 1989, Lynn put together a ten-person ownership group. The next year, Pohlad and Jacobs sued Lynn. They claimed that Lynn had unfairly gained control of the organization and was in violation of NFL rules because the league had never approved the stock transfer that gave Lynn and his group control of two-thirds of the voting stock.

The feud got worse in October of 1990 when Lynn, who had announced he was leaving the team at the end of the year to become president of the World League of American Football, appointed Roger Headrick to succeed Wheelock

Mike Lynn (left) worked alongside owner Max Winter (right) as the Vikings' general manager before becoming one of the principal owners.

Roger Headrick poses outside the Vikings' practice facility in Eden Prairie shortly after being named as the new team president.

Whitney as the team president. Headrick was from Lynn's group and was opposed by Pohlad and Jacobs.

The dispute finally ended in December of 1991, when Lynn's group bought out Pohlad and Jacobs. Jacobs and Pohlad, who had paid $25 million for Winter's stock in 1987, received more than $50 million for their shares four years later.

In 1997, NFL commissioner Paul Tagliabue and the league's finance committee finally told the Vikings' ownership group that it needed to restructure its ten-person partnership to meet the league's ownership rules. The league wanted one general partner to own thirty percent of the team's stock. The Vikings' board put the Vikings up for sale in the summer of 1997.

In February 1998, author Tom Clancy outbid Roger Headrick and San Antonio businessman Red McCombs to buy the Vikings. Clancy's bid of $200 million topped Headrick's bid of $178.5 million and McCombs' bid of $176 million.

On the day that Clancy was scheduled to be introduced as the new owner, Headrick threw everything into turmoil when he announced that he had a right to match Clancy's bid. Headrick made a new offer of $205 million.

The Vikings' Board of Directors voted unanimously to proceed with the sale to Clancy. Some of the board members even wanted to fire Headrick as team president.

Tom Clancy gleefully donned a Vikings jacket before his bid to buy the team fell apart.

Commissioner Tagliabue stepped in, and in March, he ruled in favor of Clancy's group. He also told the team's directors that they couldn't fire Headrick.

But Clancy's bid was in trouble. At the news conference where he announced that he was buying the team, Clancy got upset with me when I asked him where he was going to get the money. At the time, I didn't have any idea that he didn't have the financial ability to buy thirty percent of the team.

Clancy was going through a divorce at the time, and in the divorce papers he had listed his net worth as $13.6 million. That amount was far short of the $60 million that the league wanted from the lead investor in a $200 million deal.

Tagliabue reportedly was shocked to learn, after meeting with Clancy in May, that Clancy was planning to invest only $5 million. The Vikings owners didn't know who his partners were going to be.

In late May, Clancy faxed a letter to Tagliabue withdrawing his offer to buy the Vikings. The owners started the process again and set a July 1 deadline for bids.

This time, Red McCombs stepped up with a bid of $206 million, in addition to assuming $34 million in team debt.

Operating on a shoestring budget and led by Gary Woods, the president of McCombs Enterprises, McCombs made a fortune off the team. First, he sold Vikings Food Service for $25 million. He also received expansion money, about $50 million each for Cleveland and Houston when they joined the league in 1999 and 2002, respectively.

McCombs finally got tired of dealing with stadium issues and put the team up for sale in 2002. In early 2005, a group led by Arizona businessman Reggie Fowler bid $625 million for the team. But Fowler, like Clancy, didn't have the money to be the lead investor. Finally, Zygi Wilf, who was part of Fowler's original group, became the lead investor of the group, which paid $600 million. After owning the team for seven years, McCombs had made $360 million.

It's too early to know what kind of owner Wilf will be, but it's a positive sign that he's willing to spend money even though he doesn't know when he'll get a new stadium. Winter Park, the Vikings' training facility, needed fixing up, and he spent the money to get it done. The Vikings had the lowest-paid coaching staff and he put up the money to increase salaries.

The stadium issue haunted Red McCombs throughout his time as owner of the Vikings.

Zygi Wilf emerged from the ownership disputes to become the team's new owner in 2005.

chapter 4

HOCKEY

Mariucci and the Emergence of Gophers Hockey

The guy who made hockey at the University of Minnesota was John Mariucci. Mariucci was a native of Eveleth, Minnesota, and he played both hockey and football at the university. Mariucci was named an All-American in hockey after leading the Gophers to an undefeated season (18-0) and the national AAU championship in 1940.

After graduating, Mariucci played five seasons in the National Hockey League (NHL) with the Chicago Blackhawks—back when there weren't many Americans in the league. When his NHL career was over, he played with the Minneapolis Millers and St. Paul Saints of the United States Hockey League.

Mariucci was hired to replace Doc Romnes in 1952 as coach of the Gophers hockey team. When he was first hired, it was on a part-time basis at $2,500 per year. The Gophers squads from 1952 to 1955 were some of the best that the University of Minnesota has ever had.

In 1956, Mariucci coached the U.S. Olympic team to the silver medal at the Winter Olympics in Cortina, Italy.

Jon Waibel celebrates after scoring one of Minnesota's five goals in the 2003 NCAA championship game.

After fourteen seasons as the Gophers hockey coach, Mariucci was asked to resign in 1966. Athletic director Marsh Ryman felt that Mariucci, who was being paid $7,600 per year for coaching the team on a part-time basis, could do a better job. During his career at the university, Mariucci coached the Gophers to a 197-138-18 record, two league titles, and three appearances in the Final Four.

In 1967, Mariucci was hired by the NHL's North Stars as a scout and assistant general manager. He stayed with the team until he passed away in 1987.

In addition to his impact at the collegiate and professional level, Mariucci also played a big role in the development of high school hockey around the state. Between 1952 and 1980, the number of high school programs in Minnesota increased from around 20 to 150. Mariucci was an ambassador for the sport, and he helped to create interest in hockey by conducting coaching clinics around the state.

Mariucci's Gophers teams of 1953–55 included John Mayasich, who was the best hockey player in University of Minnesota history. Like Mariucci, Mayasich was an Eveleth native and he played on the great Eveleth teams that won four straight state hockey titles from 1948 to 1951. Eveleth, coached by Cliff Thompson, went undefeated in all four seasons and won seventy-eight consecutive games during that span. In those four state high school tournaments, Mayasich scored thirty-six goals, including a seven-goal performance in one game during the 1951 tournament.

Nobody did more than John Mariucci to elevate hockey in Minnesota at the college and high school levels. Here, in 1958, he points to the hockey side of Williams Arena, which was later renamed in his honor.

Two of Mayasich's Eveleth teammates were goalie Willard Ikola and John Matchefts. Ikola and Matchefts went on to play for the University of Michigan, while Mayasich joined the Gophers in 1951.

Mayasich and the Gophers met Ikola, Matchefts, and Michigan in the 1953 NCAA championship game. The Wolverines, coached by Vic Heylinger, won 7-3 and gave Michigan its third-consecutive NCAA title. The Gophers also reached the NCAA title game in the next season, but lost to RPI in overtime.

In 1997, the fiftieth anniversary issue of *Hockey News* named Mayasich as the Western Collegiate Hockey

Coach Mariucci poses with fellow Eveleth natives John Mayasich, John Matchefts, and Willard Ikola at the U.S. Olympic tryouts in December 1955.

John Mayasich helped Minnesota skate to the NCAA finals in 1953 and 1954.

Mariucci spent the final years of his career as a scout with the Minnesota North Stars.

Association's (WCHA) all-time best player. Mayasich was a three-time All-American. He won the WCHA scoring title in 1954 and 1955. In 1954, he set an NCAA tournament record with seven points in a game against Boston College. In 111 career games with the Gophers, Mayasich had 144 goals and 154 assists.

After his college career, Mayasich turned down a number of offers to play in the NHL and he remained an amateur. He played on the 1956 and 1960 Olympic teams, as well as the U.S. national teams that competed in world championships in 1957, 1958, 1961, 1962, 1966, and 1969.

Ikola also played for Mariucci on the 1956 Olympic team, and he played on the 1957 and 1958 national teams as well. He then became one of the top high school hockey coaches in state history at Edina. Ikola was elected to the U.S. Hockey Hall of Fame in 1990.

Herb Brooks

Other than John Mariucci, nobody did more for hockey in this state than Herb Brooks.

Brooks grew up in St. Paul and was a good player for the Gophers from 1956 to 1959. He was the last guy cut from the 1960 U.S. Olympic Hockey team. He was disappointed by that because the team went on to win the gold medal in Squaw Valley, California.

He played for the Olympic team in 1964 and 1968, and also the U.S. national team five times (1961, 1962, 1965, 1967, and 1970).

Brooks became the Gophers coach in 1972—after Glen Sonmor left to coach the Fighting Saints of the World Hockey Association (WHA)—and he really turned the university program around. The Gophers, who had reached the Final Four in 1971, struggled to an 8-24 record in 1971–72. The twenty-four losses were the most in school history. In just his second season (1973–74), Brooks coached the Gophers to their first NCAA hockey title in school history. Brooks also coached them to two more titles, in 1976 and 1979.

After the 1979 championship, he took a leave of absence from the Gophers job to coach the U.S. national hockey team. Brooks coached that team to a gold medal at the memorable 1980 Winter Olympics in Lake Placid, New York. That team included twelve players from the state of Minnesota.

Herb Brooks coached the Gophers to three NCAA titles during his seven seasons as hockey coach.

The 1974 team won the school's first NCAA hockey championship. The Gophers would win two more titles under Brooks, who left the university in 1979 to coach the 1980 U.S. Olympic team.

After the Olympics, Brooks turned down several offers to coach in the NHL and coached a Swiss team in 1980–81.

In the spring of 1981, the New York Rangers were interested in hiring Brooks as coach. Brooks' agent, Art Kaminsky, called me and asked, "What am I going to do about Herb? The Rangers want an answer and he won't give me one." I told him to call Herb's wife, Patty. The next day, Brooks accepted the Rangers' offer.

In his first season with the Rangers, he directed the team to a 39-27-14 record—the ninety-two points were the team's highest total in eight years—and the second round of the

playoffs. In his third season with the team, the Rangers had forty-two victories and ninety-three points—the most in eleven years—but they lost again in the second round of the playoffs. When they got off to a slow start in the 1984–85 season, Brooks was fired in January of 1985. The Rangers were 15-22-8 at the time and finished the season 26-44-10. It was their worst season since 1966.

In 1987, North Stars general manager Lou Nanne convinced George and Gordon Gund, the team's owners, to hire Brooks. Coaching the North Stars was Brooks' dream job—and he was working for his friends Nanne and

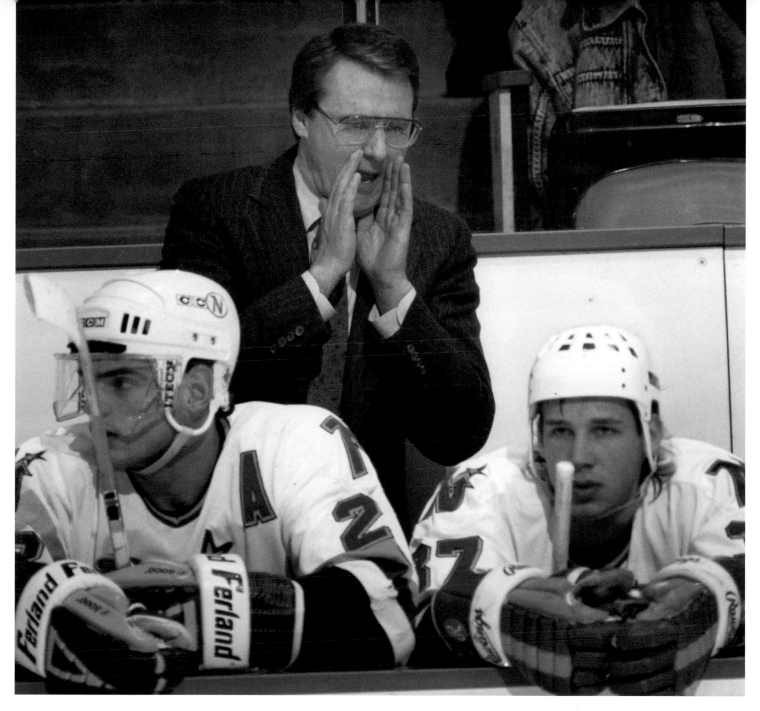

Brooks shouts instructions to his players while coaching the North Stars in 1987.

Sonmor. Unfortunately, the team had its worst season in twelve years. Minnesota finished 19-48-13 and missed the playoffs. Brooks didn't like how the ownership operated, and he expressed his sentiments to the media. As a result, he was not brought back the following season.

He coached the New Jersey Devils in 1992–93 and took them to the playoffs. Once again, he left the job after a dispute with team's owner, John McMullen. McMullen had a favorite player, Claude Lemieux, but Brooks didn't like him. McMullen told Brooks, "You don't have to play him, but

at least stop ripping him." Brooks went out and criticized Lemieux the very next day.

After coaching the French Olympic team in 1998, he coached the Pittsburgh Penguins for one season. In 2002, he was back as the coach of the U.S. Olympic team and led them to a silver medal at the Salt Lake Olympics. He then turned down an offer from the New York Rangers.

Herb was the best hockey coach I've ever seen. But he was stubborn and bounced around because he always wanted to do things his way.

The Return of the Title Years

Under coaches John Mariucci and Herb Brooks, the Minnesota Gophers put together some great teams, and established the university among the elites of collegiate ice hockey. Under another Minnesota native, Don Lucia, the Gophers accomplished the rare feat of back-to-back NCAA championship titles.

Before Lucia came on board, the Gophers were coached by another Minnesota institution. Doug Woog, who had been an All-American for the Gophers in 1965, became the Gophers coach in 1985. He led the Gophers for fourteen seasons and went on to become the winningest coach in the program's history, with a 390-187-40 record. He took six teams to the NCAA Final Four, but he never won an NCAA championship.

Coach Woog gives an earful to the referee.

Twenty years after he was an All-American player for the Gophers, Doug Woog became the team's coach.

The Gophers achieved new heights under the leadership of coach Don Lucia.

The Gophers finished with losing seasons in 1998 and 1999—their first since the 1976–77 season—and the team missed the NCAA playoffs for the first time since 1984. Gophers fans started getting upset with Woog. I've never seen a coach who had so many people for him and so many against him. There were no undecideds on Woog. Woog was a great guy who did a great job. In my opinion, he got a lot of unfair abuse.

Pat Forciea, who was a consultant to the Gophers athletic department, wanted the department to hire Don Lucia as coach. He wanted athletic director Mark Dienhart to fire Woog.

Woog had a one-year contract as coach, and Dienhart gave him the choice of coaching one more season with no guarantees beyond that or accepting another job in the athletic department (fundraising) with more security. Woog resigned as coach, and three days later, the university named Don Lucia as the new coach for the 1999–2000 season. Lucia had been coaching at Colorado College and led the team to the NCAA championship game in 1996.

Lucia has obviously done a great job at Minnesota. In just his third season (2001–02), the Gophers won the NCAA title—it was the program's first NCAA title since 1979. The Gophers were led by Jeff Taffe, who scored thirty-four goals, and John Pohl, who scored twenty-seven goals. Gophers defenseman Jordan Leopold, who scored twenty goals, won the Hobey Baker Award. Their championship victory came against Maine, with Grant Potulny putting in the winning goal in a 4-3 overtime game at the Xcel Energy Center.

The Gophers came back the next season to win the championship again and became the first team to win back-to-back titles since Boston University in 1971 and 1972. The Gophers finished in a tie for second place in the WCHA regular-season standings and then beat Colorado College in the championship game of the WCHA tournament. Minnesota then beat Mercyhurst and Ferris State at Mariucci Arena to advance to the Frozen Four. In the semifinals, the Gophers defeated Michigan, 3-2, in overtime before beating New Hampshire, 5-1, in the championship game.

Koalska celebrates his game-tying goal with a leap into the bench.

Right: The nation's top scorer during the year, Red Wing native John Pohl had a goal and two assists in the 2002 title game.

Left: Matt Koalska's goal with fifty-two seconds left in regulation sent the 2002 championship game against Maine into overtime.

Barry Tallackson puts in one of his two goals during the 2003 championship. Minnesota defeated the University of New Hampshire 5-1.

The Gophers players honor Coach Lucia with an ice bath after they won a second consecutive NCAA title.

Twice as nice in 2003.

North Stars Rising:
The NHL Comes to Minnesota

For twenty-five years, the National Hockey League consisted of just six teams: the Montreal Canadiens, Toronto Maple Leafs, Detroit Red Wings, Boston Bruins, New York Rangers, and Chicago Blackhawks. Even though ice hockey was huge in the state, we had to wait until 1966, when the league announced its plans to expand, before Minnesota got an NHL team.

Prior to that, the Twin Cities had been home to various minor-league teams from the 1920s to the 1940s and then again in the late 1950s and early 1960s. Both cities had teams in the American Hockey Association in the 1930s and 1940s, and again in the U.S. Hockey League during the late 1940s.

In December of 1959, Ben Berger, the former owner of the Minneapolis Lakers, purchased the Denver Mavericks of the International Hockey League (IHL). Berger moved them to

Minneapolis and renamed them the Millers. St. Paul already had a team in the eight-team league. The St. Paul team, called the Saints, was coached by future Philadelphia Flyers coach Fred Shero.

St. Paul won the IHL championship—called the Turner Cup—in 1960 and again in 1961. That team had stars like Ted Hodgson and John Bailey. They reached the finals again in 1962, but lost.

The Millers got to the Turner Cup finals in 1963. Following that season, both the Saints and the Millers left the IHL and joined the newly created Central Hockey League (CHL). The CHL consisted of just five teams that first year.

In the first two seasons of the CHL, the Minneapolis club was known as the Bruins and served as a farm team of the NHL's Boston Bruins. The franchise folded after the 1964–65

Harry McQueston manned the goal for the Minneapolis Millers from 1945 to 1950. Here he blocks a shot by Omaha's Gordon Heale at Minneapolis Arena in March 1949.

Future NHL coach Fred Shero led the IHL's St. Paul Saints and the CHL's Rangers in the mid-1960s.

Bob McNulty was a true hero in the effort to build a new hockey arena and bring the NHL to Minnesota.

season. The St. Paul team was the farm club of the NHL's New York franchise and was called the St. Paul Rangers. The Rangers won the CHL championship, the Adams Cup, in the league's second season of 1964–65. The Rangers played the 1965–66 season as the Minnesota Rangers and won the Central League regular-season title.

The Bruins played at the old Minneapolis Arena, which was located near Lake Street and Dupont Avenue and had a seating capacity of about 4,000. The Rangers played at the St. Paul Auditorium. In the late 1940s, the Arena, the Auditorium, and the University of Minnesota had the only three indoor hockey arenas in the Twin Cities.

On February 9, 1966, the future of professional hockey in the Twin Cities changed dramatically when the NHL announced that it was awarding an expansion franchise to Minnesota, one of six franchises joining the league beginning with the 1967–68 season.

A lot of people were surprised that Minnesota wound up with a team. The feeling was that the league would go to a bigger city in the East, such as Washington or Cleveland, rather than come to Minnesota. The other cities that received teams in the expansion were Philadelphia, Pittsburgh, St. Louis, Los Angeles, and Oakland.

The big hurdle to overcome for Minnesota to get an NHL team had always been the absence of a big-league arena. The Minnesota ownership group promised the league that they would construct a new building for the team. This also created a conflict between the cities of Minneapolis and St. Paul. Most of the money in the ownership group, which was headed by Walter Bush Jr., was from St. Paul (primarily from Robert Ridder and John Ordway Jr.). The group first went to the St. Paul City Council and said they wanted to expand the St. Paul Auditorium

Left: Before becoming the goalie for the Minnesota North Stars, the six-foot-three Cesare Maniago was the Minneapolis Bruins' net-minder in 1964–65.

The Met Center was ready for action in time for the start of the 1967–68 NHL season.

Left: Wren Blair called the shots from the North Stars' bench for the team's first two and a half seasons.

Right: Lou Nanne, "Sweet Lou from the Soo," played for the 1968 Olympic team before becoming a regular member of the North Stars.

In 1974, Bill Goldworthy became the first player on an expansion team to score forty goals in a season.

Canadian by birth, Blair was familiar with the Twin Cities; he had helped run the Minneapolis Bruins of the Central Hockey League.

The Minnesota North Stars were competitive from the start. They made the playoffs five times in their first six years, including trips to the conference finals in the opening season and again in 1970–71.

The North Stars' first season was marred by the death of Bill Masterton. Masterton, a twenty-nine-year-old rookie, suffered a brain injury in a game against California at the Met Center on January 13, 1968. He died two days later. After the season, the NHL started an annual award for leadership and sportsmanship, which they named in Masterton's honor.

Bill Goldsworthy was the first star for the North Stars. Prior to joining the North Stars in 1967, he had played just thirty-three games with the Boston Bruins—over three seasons—and had scored a total of six goals.

Goldsworthy scored fourteen goals in each of his first two seasons with the North Stars. By his third season in Minnesota, he was becoming an elite player. He was the team's scoring leader in 1969–70 with thirty-six goals. In the 1973–74 season, he scored forty-eight goals and set a team record. Nobody contributed more to the North Stars franchise in those days, when the team was selling out and winning on a consistent basis.

Besides Goldsworthy, another cornerstone of the organization in the early years was Lou Nanne, a former Gophers standout from Sault Ste. Marie, Ontario. He played four seasons of semipro hockey with the Rochester Mustangs in the U.S. Hockey League after leaving the Gophers in 1963. He was also selling envelopes for Minneapolis businessman Harvey Mackay. I was pushing for the North Stars to sign Nanne, and they finally did in March of the team's inaugural season. Nanne went on to spend his entire NHL playing career with the North Stars and was the only player to play for the team in all of its first eleven seasons in Minnesota.

Despite the emergence of players like Goldsworthy, by 1975 the North Stars had become an unexciting team. In town, they were competing with the St. Paul Fighting Saints of the WHA and they were dying. The Met Center would be only half-full for games, and the owners were losing a ton of money.

Even after the Fighting Saints went out of business (in January 1977), the North Stars weren't drawing fans and they weren't winning games. The team missed the playoffs from 1974 to 1976 and were swept in the playoffs in 1977. Big changes were needed.

to 15,000 seats so it could serve as the home for the new team. But the council turned them down. Had the St. Paul City Council agreed, the Met Center would have never been built. Ironically, a couple of years later, St. Paul decided to build the Civic Center to be a home for the Fighting Saints of the WHA.

Bob McNulty, one of the owners, and his company put up the new building for $6 million. Ground was broken in Bloomington, just north of Metropolitan Stadium, on October 3, 1966. The facility was completed in less than twelve months and was ready for opening day of the 1967–68 NHL season.

Wren Blair was hired to be the general manager and coach of the North Stars for the inaugural season. A

The Cup Runneth Empty:
From the Stanley Cup Finals to Leaving Town

The twenty-six-year history of the Minnesota North Stars was one of peaks and valleys. After the early successes, the team quickly sunk back to the bottom of the pack. Over time, Minnesota was able to field a team worthy of the State of Hockey.

In February of 1978, midway through the 1977–78 season, the North Stars made a smart move by naming Lou Nanne as the general manager. Nanne retired as a player to take the general manager position. He then named himself interim head coach and coached for the rest of the season.

The North Stars went 7-18-4 in twenty-nine games under Nanne; they finished the season with a record of 18-53-9—the worst in the franchise's eleven-year history. Because of the poor record, the North Stars earned the number-one pick in the draft. They drafted twenty-year-old Bobby Smith, the top player in junior hockey. Smith went on to be the North Stars' points leader in his rookie season. He was one of the top-three points producers for Minnesota in each of his five seasons with the team.

After the 1977–78 season, the North Stars were sold to George and Gordon Gund, who owned the Cleveland Barons. The Gund brothers merged the two franchises into the North Stars.

Nanne hired Glen Sonmor to be his assistant general manager in 1978. Eleven games into the season, Nanne named Sonmor as head coach. A year later, Sonmor coached the North Stars to a 36-28-16 record and took them to the playoffs for the first time in three seasons. They won their first playoff game since 1973 and beat the Toronto Maple Leafs in the opening round, and then Montreal in the quarterfinals. They reached the semifinals before losing to the Philadelphia Flyers, four games to one. One of the highlights of the 1979–80 regular season came in January when the North Stars defeated the Flyers, 7-1, before a sellout crowd at the Met Center and ended Philadelphia's record thirty-five-game unbeaten streak.

They had some talented players for the 1980–81 season, including Smith and rookie Dino Ciccarelli. Neal Broten,

Lou Nanne left the ice for the bench in 1978 before moving into the front office as general manager.

who won the Hobey Baker Award as college hockey's top player in 1980, signed with the North Stars right after the Gophers' season ended and joined the team for the final three regular-season games. One day after signing with the North Stars, he made his debut and scored a goal in a 6-3 win over St. Louis. Minnesota closed out the regular season with a 35-28-17 record.

Bobby Smith was a force for the North Stars as soon as he entered the league.

The North Stars opened the playoffs against their long-time nemesis—the Boston Bruins. In the series-opener, Steve Payne scored the first hat trick in franchise playoff history in the North Stars' 5-4 overtime victory in Boston. It was Minnesota's first victory ever in Boston. Prior to that game, in their thirteen seasons in the league, the North Stars were winless in thirty-five games (0-28-7) at the Boston Garden.

The North Stars went on to sweep the Bruins and then defeated the Buffalo Sabres in the quarterfinals. In the semifinals, the North Stars beat Calgary, four games to two,

and advanced to the Stanley Cup finals against the defending-champion New York Islanders. The Islanders, one of the best teams in league history, won the first three games of the series. The North Stars won Game Four at home to avoid being swept, but the Islanders closed out the series with a 5-1 win in Game Five. The Stanley Cup title was the second of four consecutive for the Islanders.

The team improved its regular-season record in each of the next two years, but they lost their opening-round playoff series to the Chicago Blackhawks in 1981–82. After posting

Coach Glen Sonmor imparts the wisdom of his three decades in hockey to Steve Payne (right) and Dino Ciccarelli (seated) in the early 1980s.

forty wins during the 1982–83 season, the North Stars beat the Toronto Maple Leafs in the first round of the playoffs before losing to the Blackhawks again.

Minnesota got its revenge against Chicago in the playoffs a year later, and then went on to beat the St. Louis Blues to set up a conference finals matchup against the Edmonton juggernaut. Wayne Gretzky's Oilers swept the North Stars in four games.

The North Stars advanced past the first round of the playoffs only once in the next six years, and twice they missed the playoffs all together.

North Stars Brad Maxwell, Tom Younghans, Dino Ciccarelli, Jack Carlson, and Kent-Erik Andersson clown around during their run to the Stanley Cup Finals in 1981.

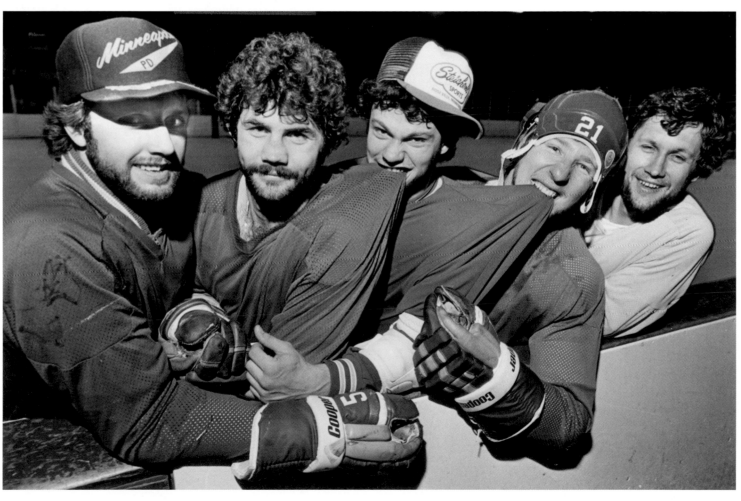

Ciccarelli set a rookie record with fourteen goals in the 1981 playoffs.

The seeds for the North Stars ultimately leaving Minnesota in 1993 had been planted three years earlier. Owners Gordon and George Gund had decided among themselves that if the Metropolitan Sports Facilities Commission would provide the funds to improve the outdated Met Center and help with season tickets from the corporate community, they would commit to remain in the Twin Cities.

In January of 1990, the Gunds requested $10 to $15 million from the commission to update the arena. They were basically laughed at. They set a deadline of February 21 for a final answer, and when the commission said no, the Gunds announced their intention to either move the team to Oakland or sell it.

By May, it looked like the North Stars were headed to California, but Nanne, who was now president of the team after ten years as the general manager, stepped up. He located Howard Baldwin and a couple of partners to buy the North Stars. As part of the deal, the Gunds were awarded an expansion franchise in San Jose, California, which would begin play in the 1991–92 season.

One of the partners in the new ownership group was Norm Green, who was also a minority owner of the Calgary Flames. It turned out that Baldwin did not have the money to make the deal work, so in June 1990, Green announced that he would purchase fifty-one percent of the team and become the team's chairman, governor, and CEO.

In the North Stars' last season in Minnesota, twenty-two-year-old Mike Modano led the team in scoring.

The North Stars opened the 1990–91 season at the Met Center in front of just 5,730 fans who witnessed the North Stars lose to the St. Louis Blues, 3-2. In January, the Montreal Canadiens came to town, and there were less than 5,000 in the building. The North Stars averaged 7,838 fans per game—the lowest attendance in the team's twenty-four years in Minnesota—during the season.

Although the North Stars finished in fourth place in the division in 1990–91, that was good enough to make the postseason. They upset division rivals Chicago and St. Louis the first two rounds of the playoffs, and then topped the Oilers in the conference finals to earn the franchise's second trip to the Stanley Cup finals. The 1991 finals between the North Stars and the Pittsburgh Penguins was the first one since 1934 in which neither team competing had won a Stanley Cup.

The North Stars won Game One in Pittsburgh, 5-4. After the Penguins tied the series with a victory in Game Two, the North Stars won Game Three at Met Center, 3-1, to take a two-games-to-one lead in the best-of-seven series.

Gordon and George Gund enjoy a rare moment of levity during their meeting with the Metropolitan Sports Facilities Commission in February 1990.

The Penguins won the next three games to win the Cup. The clinching victory for the Penguins was an 8-0 romp in Game Six at the Met Center.

After coming within two games of winning their first Stanley Cup ever, the North Stars lost twenty-four players to the San Jose Sharks in a dispersal draft as part of the expansion agreement with the Gunds from the previous year. The North Stars then selected ten players in the expansion draft.

For their eleven home games during the 1991 playoffs, the North Stars had averaged nearly 15,000 fans per game, but they couldn't sustain the momentum into the next season.

North Stars defenseman Shawn Chambers gives Pittsburgh's Jaromir Jagr a shove to clear the crease for goalie Jon Casey in the 1991 finals.

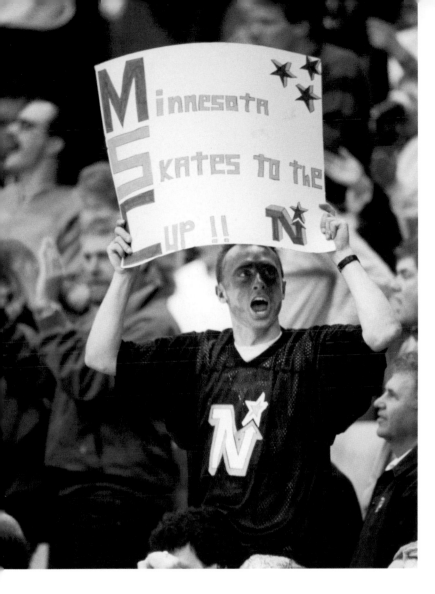

A loyal fan shows his support for the North Stars during the 1991 playoffs.

Norm Green earned the wrath of many Minnesotans when he decided to take the North Stars to Dallas.

They finished fourth in their division and were eliminated in the first round of the playoffs by Detroit.

In October of 1992, Norm Green re-signed twenty-two-year-old Mike Modano to a four-year, $6.75 million contract—making him the highest-paid player in team history. It was the fifth-largest deal in league history.

Shortly afterward, Green began talking about his team's financial problems. He said the team had lost $11 million in the little over two years since he purchased it. He needed financial concessions to keep the team in Minnesota.

With the Mall of America due to open across from Met Center, Green developed a plan to remodel the Met Center and build a small shopping center next to it. He was willing to pay for the remodeling, but he wanted a ninety-nine-year lease on the land.

Green was told by the Metropolitan Sports Facilities Commission that he would have to buy the developmental rights, but Green was not willing to pump millions into the building and also pay for the land. So, the commission blew its second chance to lock up the team and keep it in the Twin Cities.

On March 10, 1993, Green announced that he had finalized an agreement to move the North Stars to Dallas. The agreement came after a local "Save Our Stars" effort failed and a deal with the Target Center fell through.

The Minnesota North Stars played their final game at Met Center on April 13, 1993. They played their final two games on the road and missed the playoffs by one point. Their 36-38-10 record (82 points) was the team's best regular-season mark since 1985–86.

Left: One last fan soaks in the Met Center atmosphere following the North Stars' final game in Minnesota in 1993.

Wild Times:
The Return of the NHL

There wasn't a lot of support to get an NHL team back in Minnesota after the North Stars left. I remember Bill Wirtz, who owned the Chicago Blackhawks and was one of the NHL's most powerful men, telling me, "Over my dead body will Minnesota ever get another NHL team." Wirtz was furious because he believed that the previous owners of the North Stars, George and Gordon Gund, had been treated so poorly when they needed improvements made to the Met Center.

The league commissioner, Gary Bettman, did everything he could to get the Winnipeg Jets to move to Minnesota. In fact, if Bettman had been named commissioner six months earlier than he was (he was appointed on February 1, 1993), Norm Green never would have been allowed to move the North Stars to Dallas.

When the Jets were looking to relocate, Bettman stalled civic groups in other cities while hockey people in Minnesota tried to find a way to get the Jets. But an unfriendly Minneapolis City Council refused to come up with the funds necessary to bring the NHL team to the Target Center. Eventually, the Jets moved to Phoenix and became the Coyotes.

The people of St. Paul should thank the Minneapolis City Council. If the Jets had come here instead of Phoenix, St. Paul would never have been able to build a new arena to attract an expansion team.

When Minneapolis blew the chance to get the Winnipeg Jets, I was convinced we would never see pro hockey in Minnesota again. I didn't think the city of St. Paul would meet the demands of the NHL expansion committee, which

Then–Mayor Norm Coleman ceremonially drops the puck before the inaugural Minnesota Wild game in 2000.

Under the leadership of general manager Doug Risebrough (foreground) and coach Jacques Lemaire (background), the Wild reached the playoffs in the team's third season.

ruled that the St. Paul Civic Center was inadequate and demanded that a new arena had to be built.

You have to give governor Arne Carlson and St. Paul mayor Norm Coleman credit for the approval of the Xcel Energy Center. Carlson told the Legislature if they wanted their pet projects approved, they better approve the deals for the Xcel and the Minneapolis Convention Center. The St. Paul Civic Center was torn down to make room for the Xcel, which was built at a cost of $130 million.

Even when funds were made available to build a new arena, I thought it would be difficult to find anybody who would come up with the $80 million expansion fee. The expansion fee for the original North Stars franchise had been $2 million in 1966. George and Gordon Gund took over the North Stars and the mortgage on Met Center in 1978 for $6.5 million. Norm Green eventually bought out Howard Baldwin for $37 million in the summer of 1990.

Through the first five seasons, winger Marian Gaborik is the franchise's all-time leading scorer.

Wild center Wes Walz attempts to put the puck in the net against Colorado Avalanche goalie David Aebischer during the 2006 season.

When the Wild was granted an expansion franchise in 1997, more than half of the NHL teams were losing money. One East Coast financial expert advised several local businessmen not to get involved as investors in the new team. Franchise evaluators predicted that the projected revenue levels were not going to be made. They said hockey would have a hard time making it at the Xcel Center.

But Bob Naegele Jr. and his group of investors went ahead, despite the dire predictions. Besides paying the franchise fee of $80 million, the group spent $50 million of its own money to improve the arena with a terrific scoreboard. The Wild has one of the most attractive leases in the sport because the team also benefits from the concerts and other events held in the building.

The Wild won only twenty-five and twenty-six games in the first two seasons and missed the playoffs both years. In

year three, the team won forty-two games and made a deep run in the playoffs.

The Wild had the lowest payroll in the league ($20.7 million), but they finished the 2002–03 regular season with 95 points—the second-best season by a third-year team in the NHL since 1967. It was only the third time since 1970 that a team had reached the playoffs in its third season of existence.

In the first round of the playoffs, nobody gave the Wild much of a chance against the division-winning Colorado Avalance and their all-star goalie, Patrick Roy. The Wild stunned a lot of people by winning three straight games in the series—after falling behind three games to one—to win it in seven games.

In the second round, they again rallied from a three-to-one deficit in games to upset the physical Vancouver Canucks team

More than just a home for Minnesota's hockey team, the Xcel Energy Center helped to rejuvenate downtown St. Paul.

in seven games and reach the conference finals. They got swept by the Anaheim Mighty Ducks in the conference finals.

The next season, the Wild missed the playoffs by eight points, and then the entire 2004–05 season was lost to the league lockout—the first time an entire professional sports season had been cancelled due to labor issues.

Wild general manager Doug Risebrough proclaimed that the 2005–06 season would be a transition year for the team, with eleven new faces on the twenty-five-man roster. They went into the season with a payroll of $25.5 million—$13.5 million below the league's salary cap of $39 million and one of the lowest payrolls in the league. Risebrough said the team

is committed to the development of its younger players and rewarding them instead of signing free agents.

From the outset, the Wild's best player has been Marian Gaborik. As a nineteen-year old rookie in 2000–01, Gaborik led the team in scoring with eighteen goals and eighteen assists. He scored thirty goals in each of the next two seasons. In 2002, Gaborik became the first member of the Minnesota Wild to play in the NHL All-Star Game.

After setting a record for attendance by an expansion team in its first season, the Wild has continued to sell out every game. In its first four seasons, the team sold out every home game, and the consecutive sellout streak continued in the 2005–06 season.

High School Hockey in the State of Hockey

Minnesota's first state high school hockey tournament was held in 1945. That year, twenty-six schools in the state had hockey teams. Since then, the tournament has grown into the biggest high school hockey tournament in the nation. In 2006, the state featured 157 teams in two classes.

Eveleth High School, coached by Cliff Thompson, dominated the tournament in the early years. With great players like John Mayasich and John Matchefts, Eveleth was in the tournament in each of the first twelve years, and they won five of the first seven tournament titles.

Northern schools dominated the tournament for the first twenty-five years. The only southern school to win the tournament in that time was St. Paul Johnson, which won four titles (1947, 1953, 1955, and 1963).

In a ten-year span from 1957 to 1966, International Falls, coached by Larry Ross, won five state titles. A 4-3 overtime loss to St. Paul Johnson in the 1963 championship game prevented the Broncos from five consecutive state titles. The Broncos had won in 1962 and then took three in a row in 1964, 1965, and 1966. The best player on the Broncos teams was probably Tim Sheehy, who went on to play at Boston

Under coach Cliff Thompson (back row, far left), the Eveleth Golden Bears won their fourth consecutive state hockey title in 1951. John Mayasich (front row, far left) was on all four of those teams.

College and for the U.S. Olympic team in 1972. Sheehy also played eight years in the World Hockey Association and briefly in the NHL.

Ironically, it was an Eveleth native who helped the Twin Cities schools end the dominance of the northern schools. Edina High School was coached by Willard Ikola, who was a goalie on three of Eveleth's state championship teams in the early 1950s. Ikola led Edina to the state title in 1969, which was the first of eight state titles for the school. Ikola retired from coaching following the 1990–91 season. In thirty-three seasons, he led Edina to a 616-149-38 record and nineteen state tournament berths.

The 1969 tournament was played at Met Center in Bloomington—the first time the tournament was held outside of the St. Paul Auditorium. The attendance at the 1969 tournament nearly doubled that of the 1968 tournament (80,000 to 45,000). The auditorium had a capacity of 8,000, but the Edina-Warroad championship game at Met Center drew 15,063 fans. Edina beat Warroad and Henry Boucha, 5-4, in overtime.

Grand Rapids was a major force in the 1970s, winning three titles. The 1975 team, coached by Gus Hendrickson, included future Gopher and Olympian Bill Baker and future Gophers coach Don Lucia. Bloomington Jefferson won four state titles in a six-year span (1989, 1992, 1993, and 1994) under coach Tom Saterdalen. Future Gopher and NHL player Mike Crowley played on the 1992, 1993, and 1994 title teams.

The 1991 state tournament was the last single-class tournament. Duluth East won that tournament. In 1992 and 1993, the tournament was a two-class format called Two Tier. Coaches in each section ranked all the teams in their section; the top eight went into Tier I and the rest went into Tier II. After that two-year experiment, the tournament remained two-class, but the classes were based on school enrollment.

The tournament returned to St. Paul in 2001 at the Xcel Energy Center. The event continues to grow in popularity. Tournament attendance records have been broken in each of the last three years (2004, 2005, and 2006). Hockey fans are the most loyal of any sport.

At Edina, Willard Ikola became the winningest coach in Minnesota high school hockey history.

Index

Photographers' Credits

Photographs included in the book arc from the Star Tribune Photo Archives, unless otherwise noted. We would like to acknowledge the following staff photographers for the images included in these pages: Bruce Bisping, Charles Bjorgen, Duane Braley, David Brewster, Gerald Brimacombe, Russell Bull, John Croft, A. M. DeYoannes, Jim Gehrz, Carlos Gonzalez, Judy Griesedieck, Kyndell Harkness, Pete Hohn, Jerry Holt, Kent Kobersteen, Joel Koyama, Powell Krueger, Marlin Levison, Dwight Miller, Richard Olsenius, Brian Peterson, Regene Radniecki, Rita Reed, Bob Schranck, William Seaman, Richard Sennott, Paul Siegel, Jennifer Simonson, Tom Sweeney, Tom Wallace, Jeff Wheeler, Mike Zerby.